THE
PIPES & DRUMS
of THE LONDON
IRISH RIFLES
1906-2006

George Willis & George P. Willis B.Sc.(Hons)

Published by The London Irish Rifles' Regimental Association
to commemorate the Centenary of the Pipes & Drums

Designed and produced by Calder Walker Associates 2005

Editor: Alan Gordon Walker

Designer: Louise Millar

British Library Cataloging in Publication data:
A catalogue record for this book is available
From the British Library

ISBN 0-9541275-2-8

Printed by The Basingstoke Press
Basingstoke, England

Title page illustration:
The Crest of the Regimental
Association of the London Irish
Rifles as it has appeared, since
1949, on the cover of *The Emerald* –
the Association's Annual Journal.

Regimental cap badge, 1937.

Piper's caubeen badge, 1939.

Regimental caubeen badge, 1993.

Contents

Foreword

by

Major General Corran Purdon C.B.E., M.C., C.P.M.

President, The London Irish Rifles Regimental Association

I am delighted to commend this history of the Pipes & Drums of the London Irish Rifles in this their centenary year. Wherever the L.I.R. have been in the last 100 years its Pipe Band has been an integral feature. It is literally the first thing most people hear of the London Irish.

Military and civilians alike will enjoy the voyage of discovery this informative volume represents. In the context of over a thousand years of Irish piping, it comprehensively draws together for the first time the military and social history of the Band – the stories of the pipers, drummers and buglers who have played 'Garryowen' over the past 100 years. As anyone who has ever served in the Regiment or played in its Band will confirm, life is seldom dull and humour never far from the surface in the London Irish Rifles. This is certainly borne out by the many recollections included in this book.

I am proud to be the President of an Association that guaranteed its Regiment's musical heritage and traditions when it took over responsibility for the Band in 1969, after the Regiment was reduced to Company status. Nearly forty years on the Band still thrives and in publishing this volume, with its detailed chapters on uniform and repertoire, the Regimental Association has hopefully laid the foundations for the coming generations to sustain the Pipes & Drums of the London Irish Rifles for the next 100 years.

Introduction and Acknowledgements

This is the first published history of the Pipes & Drums of the London Irish Rifles in its one hundred years existence. We must emphasise it is not an official history, although the Regimental Association has greatly assisted in its preparation and are publishing it to mark the Pipe Band's Centenary.

In chronicling the band's heritage we have assumed our readers have little or no knowledge of the Regiment or its Band, so historians in general, and aficionados of the London Irish Rifles in particular, may find some of our detail obvious. But we have sought to record for posterity everything of relevance, even if the information is well known in some circles.

We hope that by including eyewitness reminiscences, anecdotal material, uniform details and repertoire notes, much more than a dry factual history emerges. In telling the story of the Band we have tried to capture the essence of the London Irish Rifles, with more than a glimpse of Cockney humour and Irish wit.

Neither individually nor jointly, have we ever researched or written a book before. Consequently we have drawn extensively on the works of others. Every effort has been made to give credit where due and detailed references are included at the end of every chapter. Nonetheless the history presented between the covers of this book is inevitably our personal view.

The writing of this book began over two years ago and we confess to never envisaging the work it would involve - particularly pursuing lines of inquiry, corroborating information, verifying personnel, places and dates. We are particularly appreciative of the help given in these respects by Tom Ball, the Curator of the Regimental Museum, and Bob Steemson his Assistant.

We are also deeply grateful to the past and present members of the Band and of the Regimental Association who responded to our requests for memories and photographs, particularly Sean Dempsey who provided the original photographs at pages 132 and 133 and whose copyright they remain. Wherever possible we have used original photographs but inevitably, over a period of 100 years, some images only remain as reproduced in newspapers and Regimental periodicals. Computer technology has been used to enhance these but the effect can be marginal. We have only used poor quality images where they verify the accuracy of the text.

An invaluable source of information was *The Emerald* - the annual Journal of the London Irish Rifles Regimental Association which was first published in September 1949. Contributors to the Journal, and its successive Editors, have created a wealth of what is nowadays called living history. We are grateful to Frances Howe for giving us unlimited access to her late husband Bill's collection of *Emeralds* and also to Ami Ibitson for her Parliamentary research.

We also wish to place on record our sincere thanks to all those who have so kindly give of their time and expertise in answering our questions, especially

Major John Fallis T.D. and Major Jim MacLeod. Particularly generous with their time in reading and commenting on early drafts were Michael Vaughan, Steve Kelly and Les Sheridan. However in the final analysis the content of the book is our sole responsibility. Although every effort has been made to be accurate and to eliminate our personal prejudices, we hope we will be forgiven for any inadvertent inaccuracies or bias in interpretation.

The conversion of our rough draft into printed reality was supervised by Alan Gordon Walker of Calder Walker Associates, and his advice and guidance was much appreciated. The book is much better for his efforts.

Finally we are indebted to our family. To Liz Willis B.Sc.(Hons.) for her design and aesthetic advice, and her sister Alison Willis M.A.(Cantab.) for new technology and Internet support. They were also relentless in correcting our grammar. Most importantly, we thank our wives Rose and Deirdre who despite describing themselves a 'piping widows' gave us time off from domestic duties to research and write this history.

George Willis and George P Willis B.Sc.(Hons)

Abbreviations Used in This Book

A.B.A.	Amateur Boxing Association
A.C.I.	Army Council Instruction
B.B.C.	British Broadcasting Corporation
B/M	Bugle Major
B.E.M	British Empire Medal
Bn.	Battalion
Capt.	Captain
Co.	Company
C.O.	Commanding Officer
Col.	Colonel
Coy.	Company
C.S.M.	Company Sergeant Major
C.Q.M.S.	Company Quartermaster Sergeant
D/M	Drum Major
Fr.	Father
H.M.	His (or Her) Majesty
H.M.T.	His Majesty's Troop-carrier
H.Q.	Headquarters
H.R.H.	His (or Her) Royal Highness
http://	Internet reference
K.O.S.B.	Kings Own Scottish Borderers
L.I.R.	London Irish Rifles
Lt. Col.	Lieutenant Colonel.
M.B.E.	Member of the Honourable Order of the British Empire
M.M.	Military Medal
M.P.	Member of Parliament
M.o.D.	Ministry of Defence
Museum	L.I.R. Museum
N.A.T.O.	North Atlantic Treaty Organisation
No.	number
O.C.A.	Old Comrades' Association
op. cit.	already quoted in this work
P.B.	Pipe Band
P/M	Pipe Major
P.O.W.	Prisoner of War
P.T.	Physical Training
Q.M.	Quartermaster
R.C.	Roman Catholic
R.I.R.	Royal Irish Regiment
R.M.S.	Royal Mail Steamer
R.M.S.M.	Royal Military School of Music
R&R	Rest and Recuperation
R.S.M.	Regimental Sergeant Major
R.Q.M.S.	Regimental Quartermaster Sergeant
R.U.R.	Royal Ulster Rifles
Rfn.	Rifleman
T.A.	Territorial Army
TAVR	Territorial Army Volunteer Reserve
W.V.S.	Women's Voluntary Service
www.	Internet reference
Y.S.	Young Soldiers

A Brief History of
Irish Pipes & Pipers

The Centenary of the Pipes and Drums of the London Irish Rifles can only be celebrated with reference to the thousand year social and military history of Irish pipes and Irish pipers, and in the wider context of British military musicians and bands.

This chapter outlines pertinent historical milestones[1] prior to the adoption of the pipes by the London Irish Rifles*.

The Great Irish War-Pipe
The Irish 'Piob Mor' (the big pipe in Gaelic[2]), also known as the Great Irish War-Pipe, was in existence from a very early date. The ancient laws of Ireland are the Brehon Laws and when these were committed to writing in the 5th century, mention was included of the 'Piob Mor' and the hum that comes from the drones[3].

The first pictorial representation of the 'Piob Mor', is to be found in one of the panels on the High Cross at Clonmacnoise, County Offaly, Ireland (dated about 910 A.D.). The sculpture[4] depicts a man playing the pipes standing on two cats.

From the 11th century onwards there is frequent mention of 'Piob Mor' in Irish literature, and many illustrations exist in medieval Irish manuscripts - noticeably[5] the manuscript of Dinnseanchus (circa 1300) where one of the decorative initial letters of a chapter includes a pig blowing double drone bagpipes with a five or six hole chanter.

In 1584 Stanihurst[6] describes the Irish war-pipes as "making use of a wooden pipe of the most ingenious structure, to which is joined a leather bag closely bound with bands. A pipe is inserted in the side of the skin through which the piper, with his swollen neck and puffed up cheeks, blows in the same manner as we do through a tube. The skin thus filled with air begins to swell and the player presses against it with his arm. Thus a loud and shrill sound is produced through two wooden pipes of different lengths. In addition to these, there is yet a fourth pipe perforated in different places, which the player so regulates by the dexterity of his fingers in the shutting and opening of the holes so he can cause the pipes to send forth either a loud or low noise."

Galilei[7] gives an excellent summary of the uses of the pipe, both in war and peace. He stated, in 1581, that bagpipes were "much used by the Irish; to its sound this fierce and warlike people march against their enemies, and encourage each other to deeds of valour. With it also they accompany their dead to the grave, making mournful sounds as to invite, nay, almost force, the bystanders to weep."

The Piping Pig, c1300.
from the medieval Irish illuminated manuscript of Dinnseanchus.
Two drone Irish 'Piob Mor' pipes are being played.

* The specific story of the Pipes & Drums of the London Irish Rifles commences with the next chapter and some readers may wish to start there.

Irish Pipers

Legend[8] has it that the nine Irish pipers who came from the hills of Bregia (County Meath) to pay homage to King Conaire the Great in 35 B.C., were "the best pipe-players in the whole world". Such was their status that they were named as Bind, Robind, Riarbind, Sihe, Dibe, Deicrind, Umal, Cumal & Ciallglind.

In 1100 A.D., the Welsh King Griffith organised a great Eisteddfod at Caerwys (Flintshire, North Wales). He had been in exile in Ireland from his youth until 1080 when he came into his lawful estate after the decisive battle of Carno. At the Eisteddfod there was a bagpiping competition and it is recorded[9] that "the prize was carried off by an Irishman, who received from the monarch a silver pipe as a reward for his skill."

The great Fairs at Carman (Leinster, Ireland) included music as well as athletics and sports. In the lists of the musicians present at the 1138 A.D. gathering, the books[10] of Leinster and Ballymore make mention of pipes and pipers.

Two excellent drawings in his book 'Image of Irelande' published by John Derricke[11] (1581) clearly illustrate an Irish piper, his pipes and importance. These detailed drawings show the bagpipe as having a chanter, a blowpipe, and two drones with a bag.

The illustration adjacent shows the piper at the head of a company of marching Irish soldiers, whilst the extract below (highlighted from a much larger drawing) shows the soldiers in retreat, leaving behind them their slain piper, with his pipes beside him. The 'pyper,' is the only individual marked on the entire drawing of over a thousand men – clearly showing the importance that was attached to a piper and his fall.

Also in the 16th century, Gordon of Straloch[12] reported Irish pipers were deemed noble by virtue of their occupation and wore Saffron dyed clothing (see page 121) to denote their social standing.

A slain Irish 'pyper' with pipes alongside. **An Irish piper at the head of a column of soldiers.**
(Both drawings are extracts from Derricke's *The Image of Irelande* (1581) and reproduced by courtesy of The Society of Antiquaries, London.)

During the English Civil War, war-pipes were carried by those regiments in Ireland who remained faithful to the Stuarts. In the records[13] may be found the names, not only of the company commanders who had pipers, but also in many cases of the pipers themselves. In 1649 these pipers were each paid 28 shillings a month – a phenomenal figure of some twenty times the average wage (equivalent to £28,000 per month nowadays). More than any drawing or saffron kilt, this showed how militarily important pipers had become.

Irish Pipers in the Service of the British Army

A unique feature of the early medieval Irish kerne (Gaelic for army or soldiers) was that it had pipers leading the soldiers into battle while actually playing their instruments. After the occupation of Ireland by the Normans in 1169, the Irish were forced to enlist men into regiments to assist the English Kings in their wars. Irish soldiers and their pipers saw much action[14] on behalf of British monarchs, including:

France (1243) for Henry III;
Gascony (1286-1289), Flanders (1297) and Falkirk (1298)
  all for Edward I;
Crecy (1346) for Edward III;
Harfleur (1415) for Henry V;
The Siege of Boulogne (1544) for Henry VIII;
Scottish Borders (1549-1550) for Edward VI;
Siege of Derry (1689) for James II.

On 22 July 1297 the Scots saw the martial effect of the pipes at their defeat at the Battle of Falkirk as the Irish line of Edward I's army advanced to the skirl of the pipes. The first record[15] of the Scots marching into battle with their own pipes was not until some seventeen years later, at Robert the Bruce's victory at Bannockburn; a victory which gave him the throne of Scotland.

Irish troops were included in Henry VIII's campaign in France. Paperwork[16] for the Siege of Boulogne (1544) still exists and includes a complete muster of the Irish

Piping for Henry VIII.
The piper is leading Irish troops fighting for the English King at the Siege of Boulogne, 1544.

(An extract from a copy of a contemporaneous painting, reproduced by courtesy of The Society of Antiquaries, London.)

contingent including its two pipers at one shilling each – twice a foot soldier's pay. The Siege also gave the first pictorial illustration of an Irish piper leading troops in the service of an English monarch. The original, large scale, picture was painted on a wall in Cowdrey House (Sussex, England) for Sir Anthony Browne on his return from the siege. The house and its paintings were destroyed by fire in 1793, but fortunately an engraving[17] had been published some years earlier.

Suppression of Piping in Ireland

While the war-pipes were alive and well on their battlefields, successive English heads of state sought to prohibit piping in Ireland. Richard II claimed[18] pipes had the ability to rouse Irishmen to acts of "insurrection" and "violence", and his Statute of Kilkenny (1366) included the prohibition of playing or even possessing war-pipes in Ireland. The English King had become paranoid that Irish pipers acted as "agents or spies on the English whereby great evils often resulted". The penalty for infraction of the Statute was death.

Prohibition was reaffirmed by Elizabeth I (though innumerable pardons appear to have been given), and again by Cromwell – but with a reduced sentence of banishment to the West Indies. After William III's victory at the Battle of the Boyne (1690) and the subsequent re-conquest of Ireland, he banned[19] "all Irish minstrels, harpers and pipers".

Having been banned from Ireland yet again, the Irish war-pipes found a home with the 11,000 strong army that Patrick Sarsfield[20] had settled in France immediately after the Siege of Limerick (1691). In the decades that followed a further 120,000 Irish sailed for mainland Europe. This became know as the 'Flight of the Wild Geese'. On 11 May 1745, at the battle of Fontenoy, war-pipes[21] led the Irish Brigade (the Wild Geese employed by the French Army) in a successful charge against Allied troops composed of English, Hanoverian, Dutch, and Austrian units under the Duke of Cumberland. The charge forced the 50,000 Anglo-Hanoverian infantry formation to retreat with about 50 per cent losses and the French followed the victory by taking most of Flanders during the next four months.

The Irish Brigade was not so lucky! The next year they were subcontracted by the French to help Bonnie Prince Charlie try to reclaim the British throne. Most of the ships conveying the force to Scotland were captured[22], and only a small number of the Irish got through. They died in the 40 minute battle that was Culloden (16 April 1746).

Clandestine Pipers in the British Army

By 1746, after centuries of suppression or prohibition, and having been on the losing side in the English Civil War, the Battle of the Boyne and Jacobite Rebellion, Irish war-pipes had effectively disappeared. (Although ingenious Irish pipers had long since developed the Uillean pipes as a replacement for the prohibited war-pipes). Henceforth Irish Regiments in the British Army avoided the use of Irish war-pipes - at least officially. Despite both active L.I.R. Battalions having pipe bands during the First World War, only one soldier (see Paddy Fogarty on page 104) was listed as a 'piper' in the nominal roll of some 9,500 men who served with the L.I.R. during the First World War.

Clandestine Irish Pipers.
Earliest known photograph of L.I.R. pipers, taken a full nine years before Irish regiments were officially allowed the pipes.
It shows two pipers, with Irish war-pipes under their arms, leading an L.I.R. Company in the 1911 Royal Progress.

(Enhanced copy of The *Evening Standard* for 22 June 1911.)

It was not until an Army Order No. 548 of 1920 that pipers[23] were legitimised for Irish Regiments. However, there are photographs[24] of pipers in Irish regiments dating from the start of the 20th Century. To conform to regulations, however, these regiments followed the example set a hundred years earlier by their Scottish counterparts of having clandestine or unofficial pipers. It is on record[25] that the Royal Scots, the oldest regiment in the British Army, with a long history of piping, regularly hid its pipers on Inspection Days in the 17th century. Indeed, it was customary in Scottish regiments for their pipers to be shown in the muster rolls as drummers or fifers.

In 1854, the War Office had grudgingly permitted the highland regiments to officially have a Pipe-Major and five company pipers. Lowland and Irish regiments had to wait until after the First World War for their pipers to be officially sanctioned[26]. In the intervening period the best the regiments could expect was that authority would turn a blind eye and a deaf ear – so long as instruments, special uniform and pay were not funded by public money. This was achieved by the extra expense being met from the officers' own pockets.

British Military Bands

Music was originally used in the British Army purely as a means of signalling instructions to the men on the battlefield or in camp usually in the form of drumbeats (see also page 92). Included in each company of about 100 men there was normally a musician who acted as the company's signaller. In time the company musician voluntarily provided the accompaniment for singing by his comrades as they moved from A to B.

In 1685 King Charles II, who had been exiled in France after the Civil War, followed French military fashion and created[27] the first British Military Band. He issued a Royal Warrant to the Grenadier Guards, authorising the maintenance of twelve hautbois in the King's Regiment of Foot Guards in London for ceremonial purposes. The hautbois was a type of oboe, though of a more powerful sound.

The Guards' band soon expanded to become a 'Band of Musik' comprising keyed bugle horns, oboes, clarinets, horns and bassoons, trumpet, serpents and 'Turkish Music'. This latter term meant the African time-beaters who played bass drum, cymbals and tambourine. The Band's role[27] was purely ceremonial and employed civilian (often foreign) musicians.

Throughout the 1700s other regiments copied the Guards and formed bands for ceremonial purposes. Many of these musicians were also civilians and not accustomed to military discipline. Records[28] exist of such musicians refusing to obey orders and being summarily dismissed from the service. The allegiances of foreign musicians were also questionable and during the Napoleonic Wars several regiments had to lay up their bands.

Some regiments avoided the problem of civilian musicians by creating their 'Band' by increasing the number of musician/signalers assigned to the component companies, and 'massing' them together when a ceremonial military band was required. The military advantage of 'massing' together the individual company musicians was also recognised. Simes[29] Military History (1768) advised that "in battle the position of Musik, drummers and fifers was in the centre of the infantry square alongside the colours. Here they should play suitably martial music to strengthen the resolve of the front line troops." Simes also advised that these musicians should help the wounded – a non combative role for bandsmen which was to evolve over the years and be formalised 150 years later as 'auxiliary medical personnel' in Article 25 of the 1929 Geneva Convention.

The 1773 inspection[30] of the Black Watch reveals the regiment had "two pipers and a very good Band of Musik". However five years later, the regimental roll[31] for the Seaforth Highlanders lists no Band of Musik but an establishment of 22 pipes and drums. When brought together, for ceremonial or military purposes, these company signallers would have constituted the first massed Pipes and Drums of the British Army.

The Military Worth of Music

Not everybody agreed that "suitable martial music strengthened the resolve of front line troops". In 1803, it was decreed from on high[32] that bandsmen "are, in the case of actual [battle] service, to fall in with their companies armed and accoutred". In the minds of those responsible for such decisions, the need for trained soldiers vastly outweighed the requirement for musicians. In short, weapons rather than musical instruments were to be taken into battle.

At the sharp end, individual regiments did not take kindly to being told how to use the musicians that were being funded directly by the regiment itself. Throughout the 1800's, regiments ignored the Order and time and time again went into battle with their bands playing.

It was not until the Boer War (1899-1902) that the Order was fully followed. All bands were stood down so as to undertake more important military tasks. It was a move that was to be repeated at the start of both the First and Second World Wars. But on each occasion the powers that be were soon forced to recognise the uplifting effect of the music on both the front line troops and the population at large.

The Age Old Piping Question

Before leaving this brief history of Irish war-pipes and British military music, the perennial question of whether the Scots or the Irish had the bagpipes first has to be addressed. Informed circles recognise this as a futile debate but the following may help from an Irish perspective:

- the three droned Scottish Great Highland Bagpipe only dates[33] from the 18th century (ancient bagpipes retrieved from the mud of the battlefield of Culloden in 1746, have only two drones);
- until the sixteenth century the Great Highland Bagpipes only had one drone[34]; whilst as early as early as 1300 the 'Piob Mor' had two (see 14th century illustration on page 6);
- there is no manuscript mention of Scottish pipes until the Exchequer Rolls[35] of 1362 detailing a payment of 40 shillings "to the King's Pipers" whilst the 'Piob Mor' has regularly featured in Irish documentation since the 11th century;
- finally, long before the Scots went to Ireland, parts of Scotland had been colonised by the Irish[36]. First in 120 A.D. under Cairbre Riada and again by the Dalradians in about 470 A.D. Many historians argue that it was inevitable that the leaders of these invasions would have taken there personal piper with them and so introduced the instrument to the Scots.

Relatively Recent History

The old 'Piob Mor' pipes of Ireland died out about the middle of the 18th century. However in 1893 the Gaelic League was founded to actively promote Irish language skills and culture, and in 1895 organised its first 'Oireachtas'. This was held over three days and like a Welsh Eisteddfod it included literary and musical demonstrations and competitions. From the outset this annual event included bagpiping competitions. The instruments used were

Two drones not three!
The London Irish Rifles playing two drone Irish War-Pipes, Rome, 1944. The two drone tradition lasted until the 1960's.

11

nostalgically called Irish War Pipes but essentially it was a Highland bagpipe with one less tenor drone so as to visually resemble the old two drone 'Piob Mor'. This was the form of pipes initially adopted by the London Irish Rifles in 1906.

After a short dalliance with the three droned ('Brian Boru') pipes (see page 15), the two drone commemoration of the old 'Piob Mor' by the London Irish Rifles continued until the 1960s. However, nowadays the instrument of choice for the vast majority of Irish pipers, including those of the London Irish Rifles, is the three droned Highland bagpipe. As far as can be ascertained, only one Irish pipe band world-wide[37] nowadays still honours the two drone Irish tradition.

Two drone piper's insignia, 1940.

References:

1. The main sources for this chapter are:
   a) *The Story of the Bagpipe* by William Grattan Flood; The Walter Scott Publishing Co., Ltd., 1911.
   b) Irish Pipes by Lieut G de M H. Orpen-Palmer (Leinster Reg.) undated article but obviously pre 1922.
2. Garaidh O Briain's analysis of Grattan Flood's The Story of the Bagpipe (www.iol.ie/~ipba)
3. op. cit. Garaidh O Briain.
4. op. cit. Garaidh O Briain.
5. *Irish Pipes* by G Orpen-Palmer (http://members.tripod/Hiedstand/phantompiper/WARPIPES.HTM)
6. op. cit. G Orpen-Palmer.
7. op. cit. G Orpen-Palmer.
8. op. cit. G Orpen-Palmer.
9. op. cit. G Orpen-Palmer.
10. op. cit. G Orpen-Palmer.
11. http://www.lib.ed.ac.uk/about/bgallery/Gallery/researchcoll/ireland.html
12. http://home.earthlink.net/~rggsibiba/html/galloglas/gallohist.html
13. op. cit. G Orpen-Palmer.
14. op. cit. Garaidh O Briain.
15. op. cit. Garaidh O Briain.
16. Public Record Office Vol XI 43.
17. An account of some ancient English historical paintings at Cowdray, in Sussex.
    by Sir John Ayloffe 'Archaeologia'; volume 3, 1775, pages 239-272
18. op. cit. Garaidh O Briain.
19. op. cit. G Orpen-Palmer.
20. op. cit. Garaidh O Briain.
21. op. cit. Garaidh O Briain.
22. op. cit. Garaidh O Briain.
23. *Irish Pipers in the British Army* by Michael Doyle (www.iol.ie/~ipba)
24. *The Irish Regiments 1683-1999* by R.G.Harris revised H.R.Wilson
    published Spellmount,, 1999; pages 97,117,130 & 193.
25. www.btinternet.com/~james.mckay/pipedrum.htm
26. www.btinternet.com/~james.mckay/scotdivm.htm
27. http://military-bands.co.uk/grenadier_guards.html
28. http://military-bands.co.uk/coldstream-guards.htm
29. *The History of British Military Bands Volume 2* by Gordon & Alwyn Turner
    published Spellmount, 1996; page 188.
30. http://military-bands.co.uk/black_watch.html
31. http://www.cabarfeidh.com/bands.htm
32. op. cit. Gordon & Alwyn Turner; page 189.
33. op. cit. Garaidh O Briain.
34. www.vivitdunkeld.com/bagpipe-history.htm
35. http://histclo.hispeed.com/act/music/music-bapipeh.html
36. op. cit. Garaidh O Briain.
37. The Deptford Irish Pipe Band, London.

The Early Days of
The London Irish Rifles

The origins[1] of the London Irish Rifles lay in the Volunteer Movement. Originally this Movement had flourished to defend the country at the time of the Napoleonic threat but had fallen dormant after Waterloo. However 1859 saw the Movement re-energised in response to fresh threats from France. A group of prominent London Irishmen resolved[2] (December 1859):

> ...... that a Volunteer Rifle Corps be at once organised according to the provisions of the Act 44, Geo. 111, cap. 54, under the title of the London Irish Volunteers, the qualifications for membership being a connection with Ireland by birth, marriage, or property; and that the corps shall consist of effective and honorary members.

On the 4 February 1860 the Government accepted the services of the London Irish Corps, but at first the Secretary of State for War would not allow the inclusion of the word Rifles in the title. However, when granted battalion status in May 1860, the London Irish were formally established as the 28th Middlesex (London Irish) Rifle Volunteer Corps. The founding fathers had prevailed!

The Regimental Band of the London Irish Rifles

The London Irish Rifles had a conventional military band almost from the outset. Records[3] show that in 1860 the Regiment gave a grand amateur theatrical performance at the Drury Lane Theatre in aid of the Band Fund. Soon 'Garryowen' was adopted as the Regimental March Past and its rendition by the Band at the 1870 Annual Inspection was described as "excellent" by *The Daily News* (21 July).

(ABOVE)
The 1860 shako badge.
The evolution of the badges
and uniforms of
The London Irish Rifles is
detailed on pages 121 to 134.

(RIGHT)
**The Regimental Band of
The London Irish Rifles.**
St. Patrick's Day 1906
and no bagpipes in sight!

Throughout the Victorian era there were some sixty "band and drummers" shown on the published annual Regimental roll. By 1906 this number had fallen to less than 35 musicians and the military band was to remain at about this level until it was stood down in the early 1930's (see page 29). There were also some thirty "buglers" (further details on page 95).

The Boer War 1899-1902

The London Irish Rifles was founded as a Volunteer Force to defend the Country and not to serve abroad. As such as it did not serve as a Regiment in the Boer War[4], but when the two Boer Republics declared war on 12 October 1899, the entire Regiment volunteered[5]. From these volunteers, L.I.R. contingents were selected[6] for the City Imperial Volunteers and the Volunteer Service Companies of the Royal Irish Rifles. Other London Irish Rifleman found their way into the Imperial Yeomanry, the Middlesex Regiment and Royal Dublin Fusiliers.

The men of the London Irish distinguished themselves throughout this war, and in recognition of the contribution made by 208 of its members who served, the London Irish Rifles were awarded their first Battle Honour, South Africa 1900-1902.

Irish Regiments take up the Pipes

Although earlier in the 19th century there had been the occasional 'piper to the commanding officer' in Irish regiments, it was[7] only in 1891 that a band comprising eight pipers accompanied by drummers was established by 2nd. Battalion Princess Victoria's (Royal Irish Fusiliers). The 'Irish war-pipes' used by the Irish Fusiliers were essentially Highland pipes, but just had two drones so as to resemble the 'Piob Mor' of old (see page 5).

The Prince of Wales's Leinster Regiment and The Royal Inniskilling Fusiliers followed suit early in the 20th century.

The Pipes come to the London Irish Rifles

Conceptually, Irish bagpipes came to the London Irish Rifles with the appointment of Lt.-Col. Hercules Pakenham as its Commanding Officer in November 1906. An Irishman, who was a direct descendant of the First Lord Longford (Master of the Irish Rolls for Charles I), Lt.-Col. Pakenham was the first C.O. not to have first been a company commander in the Regiment. With substantial Regular Army experience in the Grenadier Guards and then the Royal Irish Rifles, he was appointed to the London Irish to manage the major upheaval that would result from reforms being formulated by the Secretary of State for War.

Haldane's Territorial and Reserve Forces Act (1907) established a Territorial Force directly accountable to the War Department in place of the quasi-autonomous Volunteer and Militia Battalions. The Regiment became the 18th (County of London) Battalion The London Regiment (London Irish Rifles). The designation of it soldiers was changed from private to riflemen and plans were announced to forcibly move the Regimental H.Q. from the Strand (see page 88). Apart from overseeing all these changes, Lt.-Col. Pakenham also set about enhancing the 'Irishness' of his Regiment including the introduction of Irish war-pipes.

Three ranks of pipers, 1911.
An enhanced extract from a poor quality photograph of the Regimental Military Band which had pipers in its back ranks.

(RIGHT)
Col. Hercules Pakenham
who brought the concept of a
Pipe Band to the L.I.R. when
appointed its C.O. in 1906.

(FAR RIGHT)
Pipe Major Albert Starck
was not only the first Pipe Major
of the London Irish Rifles, but he
was also the principal bagpipe
maker for the British Army.

(photograph reproduced by permission
from the book *Highland Bagpipemakers*
by Jeannie Campbell.)

Early in his command, Lt.-Col. Pakenham enrolled an established piper called Albert Starck to serve as the C.O.'s piper, and to train volunteers from the ranks as pipers. Unfortunately the majority of the Regiment's records for 1907-8 concern the upheaval caused by the Haldane Reform', and no records can be found of drills, concerts, camps or parades and the involvement of pipers therein during this period.

Although there are no pipers present in the Band photograph of 1906 (see page 13), many military historians are of the view that the London Irish had the pipes by 1906. A more balanced view[8] however is that "..... pipes were introduced by 1906-07". This estimate is consistent with the first public appearances by London Irish pipers in 1909 - two years having been spent making pipers from novices (by means of weekly practices). The Band's appearances at the 1909 Regimental Smoking Concerts were billed as "The Band and Pipes of the London Irish Rifles". On other occasions in 1909, references are made to "The Regimental Pipers".

Above a caption "The London Irish Rifles on their way to take up position in Trafalgar Square", a newspaper photograph[9] of the Coronation of King George V in June 1911, shows a company of the Regiment led by two pipers (see photograph on page 9). Another newspaper[10] report of the occasion stated "the Irish bagpipe band attached to the Rifles seized the opportunity, and skirled and droned effusively". A fuzzy photo of the July 1911 Camp at Shorncliffe (see page 14) suggests that the L.I.R. had at least twelve pipers, more than enough to constitute an "Irish bagpipe band".

Pipe Major Albert Starck and 'Brian Boru' Pipes
Albert Starck (1874-1955) was the first Pipe Major of the London Irish Rifles and was descended from a family[11] that the composer Handel brought over from Germany in the 18th century to make woodwind instruments for his musicians. Albert worked for his father in the family business Starck & Co., and by the time he became involved with the LIR, the company was already a well established musical instrument makers and the principal bagpipe manufacturer for the British Army.

Initially all the Irish regiments played the two drone 'Irish war-pipes' to underscore their Irish identity, but the limited musical scale of the simple chanter caused difficulties when playing with the other instruments of the regimental band. In the early 1900's, Albert's father Henry was involved[12] with William O'Duane in developing bagpipes with a chromatic scale. This was achieved by adding additional holes to the chanter which were operated by keys. In 1908, Henry Starck patented this design and named them 'Brian Boru' pipes, after the man acknowledged as the High King of Ireland by every lesser ruler between 1002 and 1014 A.D. These pipes were made by the family company and had three drones – bass A, tenor A, and baritone E.

Despite being known in army circles as 'pigskin pianos', 'Brian Boru' pipes were enthusiastically taken up by the pipers in the regimental bands of the Irish Regiments, including of course the London Irish Rifles. By the start of the First World War the 1st. Bn. L.I.R. was playing 'Brian Boru' pipes. However during the War, Irish Regiments started to revert to using the 'traditional' Irish war-pipes. As early as 1915 the 2nd. Bn. L.I.R. was using two droned Irish war-pipes with the simple keyless chanters. After the First World War, only the Royal Inniskilling Fusiliers were to remain loyal to the 'Brian Boru' pipes. These pipes were to be the 'Skins' instrument of choice until they were merged with the Royal Irish Fusiliers and the Royal Ulster Rifles in 1968, whereupon the all pervasive three droned Highland pipes were adopted.

At the start of the Second World War Albert Starck visited the L.I.R. in Kent. By then he was in his late sixties but still making bagpipes. He talked of his time as the founding father of the Pipe Band and his First World War experiences as a piper with the Regiment. He gave the Battalion a recital on his 'Brian Boru' pipes - a sound that had been captured[13] many years earlier on his early recording of the 'Rakes of Mallow' and 'The Wearing of the Green'.

When Albert died in 1955, the firm passed to his son Henry, who was to continue in the bagpipe business until his death in 1988.

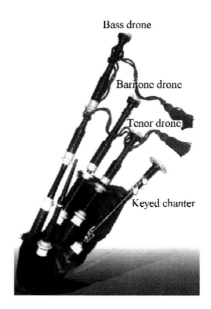

'Brian Boru' Bagpipes.
First produced, in 1908, by Henry Starck & Co. The keys on the chanter give the pipes a full chromatic scale.

References:

1. The main sources for this chapter are:
    a) *The Regimental Centenary* published by the London Irish Rifles Regimental Association, 1959.
    b) *The Irish Regiments 1683-1999* by R.G.Harris revised H.R.Wilson
       published by Spellmount, 1999.
2. op. cit. *The Regimental Centenary*. 1959; page 27.
3. *The Emerald* No.58; page 11.
4. op. cit. *The Regimental Centenary*; page 29.
5. op. cit. *The Regimental Centenary*; page 29.
6. op. cit. R.G.Harris; page 251.
7. *Irish Pipers in the British Army* by M.Doyle www.iol.ie~ipba/army.html
8. op. cit. R..G.Harris; page 251.
9. *The Evening Standard* 22nd June 1911.
10. *The Evening Standard* 24th June 1911.
11. *Henry Starck* by J. Campbell (www.iol.ie~ipba/stark.htm)
12. op. cit. J. Campbell.
13. http://www.besmark.com/irish.htm (this recording is clearly of Pipe Major Albert Starck on
    'Brian Boru' pipes despite the wrong initial and the mis-spelling of his surname).

The First World War (1914-18)

Near the Front, 1915.
The Pipes & Drums of the 1st.
Battalion of the London Irish Rifles,
identifiable by the three droned
'Brian Boru' pipes with their keyed
chanters.

In the space available here, it is impossible to do justice to, or even outline the history of the Regiment during the First World War. Fortunately the salient points are detailed in *The Story of the London Irish Rifles*, published by the Regimental Association in 1984 to commemorate the 125th Anniversary of the Regiment.

Much has been written about the London Irish Rifles and the First World War, particularly regarding the battle of Loos. Here the London Irish, when sent over the top towards the enemy on the morning of 25 September 1915, produced a football and as they charged[1]:

> they kicked it before them across a plain, as flat, grassy and as bare of cover as the upper stretches of Wimbledon Common. A game of football on the borderline between life and death! What a fantastic concept. No wonder the French troops observing were astounded by the spectacle and said "it is magnificent but it is not war!"

However, despite the millions of words describing the heroics of the London Irish Rifles, very little has been published about its Pipes and Drums during the First World War. This is not so surprising, as Irish regiments were still not officially allowed to have pipers, and their presence was often concealed on the roll (see page 8).

So good was the concealment of clandestine pipers that when, based on official records, a First World War Pipers' Memorial was conceived, only one Irish regiment was commemorated as having pipers.

The Longueval Great War Pipers' Memorial

More than 1000 Allied Army pipers were killed and many more were wounded during the First World War, but for nearly a century no memorial existed to these men. This omission was rectified[2] by the unveiling of the Great War Pipers' Memorial at Longueval, France in 2002.

The intention of the monument is to pay tribute[3] to the men "who when the whistle blew went over the top with the rest of the men. Their defiant display of unshakable bravery and their stirring tunes inspired their comrades and struck fear into the hearts of the enemy." The six foot high monument sculptured by Andy De Comyn depicts a piper in full battle dress, kilt and tin helmet climbing up and over the parapet of a trench playing his pipes. The statue is surrounded by a low Wall of Remembrance accommodating the crests of the regiments that lost pipers. Initially the Dublin Fusiliers were the only Irish regiment to have its pipers commemorated, because it had specifically recorded pipers and any deaths in action on their nominal roll for the First World War.

Following further research into the Irish Regiments engaged in the First World War, the names and regiments of Irish pipers killed during the conflict were made available to the Organising Committee of the Pipers Memorial. It was subsequently agreed that the Wall of Remembrance be modified to accommodate the twelve crests of the regiments initially omitted including that of the London Irish Rifles. The formal Installation of the Irish Regimental Crests on the Wall of Remembrance was held at Longueval on Saturday 18th October 2003.

(LEFT)
Installation of the Crests of the Irish Regiments
who lost pipers during the First World War.
Major General Purdon officiates at the Pipers' Memorial, Longueval.

(BELOW)
London Irish Rifles Crest
as depicted on the wall of the Pipers' Memorial.
Photograph © Ian Alexander

About to see action in France, Jordan, Egypt, Macedonia & Palestine.
The Pipe Band of the 2nd. Bn. L.I.R. in 1915, easily identifiable by the keyless chanters of their two droned Irish war-pipes.

Piping Pals from Haverstock Hill

The Pipes and Drums of the London Irish were recruited in circumstances typical of the First World War, where an entire group of 'Pals' would be enrolled in the same regiment. Over fifty years later Leslie Marston, M.M. (Corporal 1914 2nd. Bn. Signal Section) recalled[4]:

> The pipers and drummers the Haverstock Hill Company of the Catholic Boys Brigade became, in 1914, the 2nd. Bn's Pipe Band. They were joined by Pipe Major Moloney seconded from the 1st. Bn. Thereafter "Are you ready Mr. Moloney?" from the R.S.M. or even the C.O. became one of the Battalion's catch phrases.

Piping Pals from Barking

The ranks of the 1st. Bn.'s Pipe Band, was augmented[5] at the start of the War by young men from the flute band of the Barking Catholic Boys Brigade. Those who retrained as pipers easily made the transition from keyed flute to the keyed chanter of the 'Brian Boru' pipes (see page 16) being played by the 1st. Bn. at that time. One such musician was Dick Marshall who, as well as becoming a piper with the L.I.R., was also for a time bugler to General French, the C-in-C of the British Expeditionary Force in France.

The First Piper on the Radio

After the War, Dick Marshal started the Canning Town Brian Boru Pipe Band. With the keyed chanter's ability to play any tune, this band was popular with a wide audience and its fame soon came to the notice of Radio 2LO in London - Britain's first radio station and the predecessor to the BBC.

Although the human voice was first transmitted by radio waves in 1906, radio stations providing news and entertainment were a post First World War concept. For its first Hogmanay broadcast in 1922 Radio 2LO engaged Dick to pipe in the New Year. He thus became the first piper on radio anywhere.

Reaction to the broadcast was favourable and one reviewer[6] said that "the bagpipe solo must have been a joy to any Scotsman listening in". However few would have appreciated that the tunes played that midnight would not be possible on the limited chanter of highland pipes.

Trench warfare
plumbs new depths, as Piper Gibbons provokes friend and foe alike with his Irish repertoire.

(drawn by Harry Tyers who fought alongside the piper at Festubert, 1915.)

Pipers in the Trenches

Two veterans of the First World War recalled[7] bagpipes being used against the enemy at Festubert, France 1915. Stanley Hopkins wrote:

> At Festubert E.E.Gibbons, one of the members of our famous Pipe Band, played his pipes and the Saxons retaliated by ringing a bell. Piper Gibbons later took part in, and survived, the battle of Loos.

If a picture is worth a thousand words, then Harry Tyers' contemporaneous cartoon of this event suggests both sides of No Man's Land regarded Piper Gibbons (or at least his piping) as a 'Horror of War'.

Piper Gibbons himself recalled[8] that at the time he was the only piper with a complete set of pipes. Another Loos Survivor remembers[9] Pipers Gibbons and Carvell playing the march 'Father O'Flynn' to lead the troops back from the line for a rest in the billets.

Pipers as Fighters

Whilst the rank of piper was never officially ascribed to a specific individual, there is one instance where a newspaper[10] described the heroics of a certain Piper Raun. During the Second Battalion's boxing finals at Sutton Veny (1915), the traditional A.B.A. contests – three rounds each of three minutes – were augmented by a 'special' six round contest between a Rfn. Hounsome and Piper Raun. At six rounds, this was clearly a contest outside of the A.B.A. rules, and the following newspaper extract reflects its nature as a grudge match:

> .... some fast and clever boxing was seen. Blood was drawn in the second round and frequent visits to the mat and ropes by both men proved the earnestness of each boxer. After six earnest rounds Piper Raun was declared the winner.

Irish War-Pipes Warm the Heart; Fire the Blood!

The pipes and drums did appear to have an uplifting effect in that terrible conflict the First World War. When talking over old times, the Old Comrades of the London Irish Rifles would reminisce how they loved marching behind the Band. One First World War veteran recalled[11]:

> Throughout the training in England, even more so on active service abroad, the pipers were an inspiration and a tonic, especially on long route marches. The sound of the pipes invariably brought out the inhabitants of the villages and towns to watch us go by. At the end of a long and tiring march the Command 'March to Attention' followed by the pipers striking up 'Garryowen' brought all ranks up to the final effort of the day or even night.

More poetic testimony[12] published in 1916 reported:

> The London Irish [at the Somme] are also able to warm their hearts and fire their blood with the strains of the ancient Irish war-pipes. This old barbaric music has magic in it. It transforms the Gael. It reawakens in the depths of their being, even in this twentieth century, impressions, moods, feelings, inherited from a wild untamed ancestry for thousand of years, and thus gives them, more than strong wine, that strength of arm and that endurance of soul which makes them invincible.

The brief eight page *History of the London Irish Rifles*, published in 1916, also recorded[13] the uplifting effect of the pipes:

> The London Irish have been in the thick of it ... their spirits never left them. They took their Irish pipers out to France with them. On one occasion the London Irish Rifles were ordered to hold on to an exceptionally difficult place ..... The London Irishmen were tired, having been long in action, but they settled grimly to their task. Suddenly there rose up from the trenches the familiar strains of 'St. Patrick's Day', given with vigour by the pipers. A new spirit entered into the men and a roar of cheers went down the line. Presently the 'Minstrel Boy' was played and rifle fire was redoubled .

Father Lane-Fox

Over the years there has always been a close relationship between successive Bands and the Regiment's padres. Some even came to be regarded as honorary Band members - provided they stood their round.

The clergy at war are usually unsung heroes; little is known of their actions and their relevance is often questioned. In 1915 there was correspondence in the *Spectator* periodical concerning[14] whether army chaplains were "of any earthly good at the Front". One participant in the debate sent a letter she had received from her son in the trenches. He wrote:

> There is a man of great influence out here. He is a priest attached to an Irish Regiment. He insists on charging every time with the men, and no one dare protest. He is the absolute idol of the regiment.

In 1916 it was revealed[15] that:

> This was Father Lane-Fox, the chaplain to the London Irish, who joined the famous charge at Loos, giving the last rites to those who fell and arriving at the German trenches with the foremost. And many of the men will tell you that they are the Lucky Irish because of the comfort and reassurance they derive from the prayers and actions of their self-sacrificing chaplain.

The London Irish teach the Irish Guards the Pipes

The Irish Guards did not have a pipe band until 1916, a full ten years after the London Irish took to the pipes. An important piping footnote to the First World War is that the first twelve pipers of the newly formed Guard's Band were trained[16] by pipers of the London Irish Rifles.

Demobilisation, Honours and the Toll

The War may have ended on 11 November 1918, but the last of the London Irish did not leave continental Europe until 10 May 1919. The Regiment was officially welcomed home by the Mayor of Chelsea on 12 June 1919 at the Duke of York's H.Q. By then, however, the majority of the Regiment had been demobilised with a curt[17] "Thank you, Good Morning".

The Regiment's First World War actions yielded twenty-four battle honours including Loos, The Somme 1916 & 1918, Messines 1917, Ypres 1917, Cambrai 1917, France & Flanders 1915-18, Jerusalem, Palestine 1917-18. These honours and other evidence suggest that the regiment was continually in the thick of battle for over three years.

The causalities sustained by the London Irish during the First World War were: killed 1,016; wounded 2,844; captured 303.

The Regimental Band played with the L.I.R. 3rd. Battalion who served in England as a reserve force during the First World War.

References:

1. *The Emerald* No.29 page 40.
2. www.ifrance.com/pipersmemorial/
3. www.heritage.scotsman.com/cfm/heritagenews/headlines
4. *The Emerald* No 27; page 6 Leslie Marston M.M.
5. Display in L.I.R Museum.
6. *Popular Wireless Weekly*; 6th January 1923.
7. Harry Tyers' Unpublished Diaries and Stanley Hopkins' Unpublished Memoirs, both in the LIR Museum.
8. *The Emerald* No.19; Piper E.E.Gibbons.
9. op. cit. E.E.Gibbons.
10. *The Emerald* No.21; page 32.
11. op. cit. Leslie Marston.
12. *The Irish at the Front* by Michael MacDonagh published 1916.
13. *A Brief history of the Regiment and of its work at the Front*; published by the London Irish Rifles; page 4.
14. *The Emerald* No.39; page 39.
15. op. cit. Michael MacDonagh.
16. *Badge Backings and Special Embellishments of the British Army* by D.G.Walls page 119; published by the UDR Benevolent Fund.
17. op. cit. Leslie Marston.

Remembrance

The London Irish Rifles 1914-18 War Memorial.

Approximately three quarters of a million British subjects died during the First World War and, due to an official refusal to allow repatriation of the dead, millions of bereaved Britons were left with no physical focus for their grief or remembrance. The sheer scale of the loss and the effect it had on cities, towns and villages resulted in communities all over Britain raising funds and erecting memorials to their fallen.

War Memorials

It is estimated[1] that there are some 54,000 war memorials throughout the UK, the vast majority dating from the First World War.

Prior to the Boer War (1899-1902) commemoration of the war dead was the exception rather than the rule. Many of the 20,000 British who died during the Boer War were volunteers and some communities (including the London Irish Rifles) raised memorials to the actions of their volunteers who served. The inscriptions tended to include details of all those who had seen service – both[2] the casualties and those who survived.

The London Irish Rifles' War Memorial

The Memorial to the 1016 members of the London Irish Rifles who were killed or missing presumed dead during the First World War was unveiled by the Duke of Connaught (see page 28) on 26 May 1923.

In 1949 the London Irish Rifles' War Memorial was redesigned[3] to include the names of the 747 members of the Regiment killed or missing presumed dead during the Second World War. The opportunity was also taken to add two bronze figures on pedestals at the foot of the main dedication. At the time these figures were called the 'Footballer of Loos', (representing the soldiers of the First World War) and a 'London Irish Rifleman in Action', (representing the soldiers of the Second World War). These statues were soon being called 'The Man of Loos' and 'The Son of the Man'.

The redesigned Memorial was dedicated on 25 September 1949.

Remembrance Ceremonies and Services

The First World War also saw the emergence of 'remembrance ceremonies and services' in preference to 'victory parades'.

Although 11th November 1918 saw the end of hostilities, it was not until the Treaty of Versailles, 28th June 1919, that peace was a reality. The British Government had been working on plans for a Peace Day to mark this for some time. The Lloyd-George's vision was for a simple event but this was rejected[4] by his coalition cabinet. who favoured a victory style celebration and this was arranged for 19 July 1919.

Lloyd George was to prevail however in having a tribute to the dead. He had been taken with the French plan to have in the Paris Victory Parade troops marching past a great catafalque and saluting in honour of the dead. Lloyd George asked the architect Edwin Lutyens to come up with a design for a British equivalent to be temporarily assembled for the London Parade to salute. Within hours he had produced a set of working drawings of a 'cenotaph' (ancient Greek meaning literally 'empty tomb').

The public's response to celebrating the peace was mixed. Many ex-service men boycotted the day and the strength of feeling can be gauged from the following statement[5] by the Norwich Ex-Servicemen's Federation:

> Our pals died to kill militarism, not to establish it here. We have had militarism burned into us, and we hate it. This Federation, which consists of nearer 4,000 men than 3,000, has decided that they will take no part in the celebration of this mock peace.

The most serious disruption came in Luton, where there was bad feeling over the local Council's refusal to allow discharged soldiers to hold a remembrance service, for their fallen comrades, in a local park. On 'Peace Day' the Town Hall was broken into and a bonfire was made of papers. The *Daily Express* reported[6]:

> Peace has brought disaster to Luton. They are now without a town hall, half of the police force of the town is on the sick list, nearly all the members of the fire brigade are down with injuries, more or less serious, and there is a bill of damages estimated at more than £200,000.

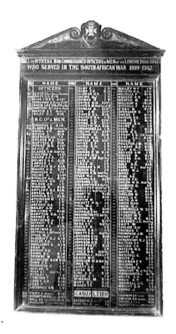

First Regimental Memorial detailing all who served in the Boer War and the casualties sustained. Note: The Regimental badge at the top of the memorial is the L.I.R.'s Victorian crest of a crowned harp on a Maltese cross (see page 92).

Design for the Updated War Memorial, 1949.
To commemorate the 1763 members of the London Irish Rifles who were killed in the service of their Country during both World Wars.

Although the temporary Cenotaph (designed and built of wood and plaster in two weeks) was intended as a minor detail in the Peace Day Celebration, it caught the public's imagination. This understated and abstract monument overnight became the symbol of British grief. It allowed the population, as a nation and separately, to remember its armed forces and the 750,000 individuals who never came back. It was reported[7] that:

> .... just before the arrival of the procession, a lady, richly attired in the deepest mourning, emerged from the crowd. Silence immediately fell upon the huge assemblage. Slowly advancing to the Cenotaph, she reverently laid a beautiful wreath at its base. She remained for a few moments with head bowed in sorrow and pride before disappearing among the people.

At the end of 'Peace Day', the base of the temporary Cenotaph had been spontaneously covered[8] in wreaths to the dead and missing.

By the first anniversary of the 1918 Armistice the powers-that-be still had not got the message and there was no national ceremony of remembrance[9]. This did not stop the crowds thronging to the now somewhat dilapidated wooden Cenotaph to observe[10]:

> two minute silence ... so that, in perfect stillness, the thoughts of everyone may be concentrated on reverent remembrance of the glorious dead.

Such was the extent of public enthusiasm for the construction it was decided that the Cenotaph should become a lasting memorial, and the permanent stone Cenotaph was unveiled by King George V on 11th November 1920. The first National Remembrance Day Service took place at the Cenotaph on 11th November 1921. The Service has changed little over the years from that first used then. Hymns are sung, prayers are said and a two minute silence is observed. Official wreaths are laid and the ceremony ends with a march past of war veterans; a poignant gesture of respect for their fallen comrades.

Nowadays, at 11 a.m. on the Sunday nearest the 11th November, similar ceremonies and services of Remembrance are held at war memorials throughout Britain, including that to the fallen of the London Irish Rifles.

We shall remember them.
Past and present members of the London Irish Rifles, their families and friends gather every Remembrance Sunday to remember those who have served and have passed on.

25

(LEFT)
Dud Corner Cemetery near Loos, 1981.
Apart from some 1700 graves, it also contains the memorial to 20,000 men who fell in the area and have no grave.

(BELOW)
Loos Sunday, 1932
at the London Regiment War Memorial, outside the Royal Exchange.

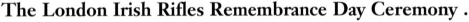

The Regimental Day of Remembrance

The London Irish Rifles has its Regimental Day of Remembrance on the Sunday prior to the 25th September - the anniversary of the Battle of Loos. The location and nature of the event varies, but the advent of cheap travel has resulted in closer ties with the people of Loos-en-Gohelle. Joint ceremonies in both countries tend to be a combination of remembrance of sacrifice and a celebration of freedom (see also pages 66 and 78).

The London Irish Rifles Remembrance Day Ceremony .

On Remembrance Sunday in November, the London Irish Rifles firstly parades and observes the national two minutes silence at 11 a.m. Then the extended L.I.R. community assembles before the Regimental War Memorial in the drill hall. The 'Last Post' is sounded by the Bugle Corps and a piper plays the lament. An absolute silence descends on the gathering for a period of solemn remembrance of its dead commences. Two minutes later this is brought to an end by a bugler sounding 'Reveille'. By tradition, throughout the land, this is followed by the 'Exhortation':

> They shall grow not old as we that are left grow old, age shall not weary them, nor the years condemn. At the going down of the sun and in the morning, we shall remember them ....
>
> **....... We shall remember them.**

References:

1.   by the Imperial War Museum (http://www.iwm.org.uk/collections/niwm/.)
2.   for example Latimer, Berkshire; (http://met.open.ac.uk/genuki/big/eng/BKM/Military/Boer_War/Latimer/)
3.   *The Emerald* No.1; page 1.
4.   http://www.aftermathww1.com/peaceday.asp
5.   quoted in *The Story of the Cenotaph* by Eric Homberger, in *Times Literary Supplement*, 12 November 1976.
6.   The *Daily Express*; 21 July 1919.
7.   The *Sunday Times*; 20 July 1919.
8.   http://www.bbc.co.uk/religion/remembrance/history/cenotaph.shtml
9.   http://www.veteransagency.mod.uk/remembrance/remem_1.htm
10.   http://www.dva.gov.au/commem/rememb/rem_silence.htm

The Calm Before the Storm

In 1920 the Regiment was reconstituted as a Battalion with the designation the 18th London Regiment (London Irish Rifles).

The next 15 years were to be what was described[1] as "the lean years". Recruitment was slow and the strength of the Battalion was never very high. Having experienced the bitterness and suffering[2] of 'the War to end all wars', the population was weary and understandably saw no need for continued high level expenditure on defence. Drastic cuts were made during this period in defence expenditure, and the Territorial Army was particularly hard hit. This was particularly so after the Great Depression (which commenced 1929) when there was a drive for national economies.

The pipes' survival, during the very difficult inter war years, was to an extent guaranteed by Army Order 548 of 1920 which authorised (and funded) one sergeant piper and five pipers per Irish regiment. With the traditional military brass band already reactivated as the Regimental Band, there were to be no more than eight L.I.R. Regimental pipers for the next ten years or so.

Apart from the annual Loos Commemoration and Remembrance Day Parades, public appearances by the Regimental Band (and its pipers) were few and far between. It would appear (see page 29) that there were difficulties in getting them to parade.

Operation Ulster

By 1930 it had become a source of considerable irritation that, whilst their counterparts at the London Scottish enjoyed periodic summer camps in Scotland, the London Irish had never, in their then 70 year history, been allowed to undertake exercises in Ireland. Repeated approaches through various channel always resulted in a categoric refusal, either on grounds of cost or the unstable political situation in the island of Ireland.

Col. Mulholland, the C.O. of the L.I.R., mentioned this to Lord Craigavon, the then Prime Minister of Northern Ireland during a chance meeting in 1930. As a result[3] the Colonel was invited to Belfast to discuss the idea further. Key issues were easily resolved in meetings with the Province's Prime Minister, its Chief Constable and the Lord Mayor of Belfast. Subject to War Department approval, the Regiment was guaranteed "the freedom of County Down and County Antrim" the moment it landed in Belfast.

This cut no ice with the War Department. So Col. Mulholland used the opportunity of that year's Annual Report as an opportunity "to pour his heart out" about the opposition of the War Department to the proposed L.I.R. Ulster camp. By custom the Annual Report was a face to face presentation and discussion with the Regimental Hon. Colonel, H.R.H the Duke of Connaught. The Duke's response to the Colonel's plea is recorded[4] as "Don't worry Mulholland, it would be a sad state of affairs if the Senior Field Marshal of the Army cannot have his request complied with."

Needless to say the Duke prevailed and on 13 July 1931 he inspected the Regiment before it entrained for its first Ulster Summer Camp.

The First Summer Camp in Northern Ireland, 1931.
The Band leads 315 L.I.R. men through Donaghadee. Eight 'guest' pipers are easily identified by their shining caubeen badges.

Col. Mulholland was to later say[5] that pages could be written about the many incidents of this Ulster tour but "looking over the photographs of this tour one stands out, proving the draw of the pipes". His detailed recollection[6] is as follows:

> Another amusing incident that day was that three small boys attached themselves to us as we left Newtownards, two of them bare-footed. They were still with us when we reached Donaghadee. As it was noted that the seats of their pants were somewhat worn, they were re-clothed and also given food and boots. We sent them back by transport, and they were delighted with their day's outing. The distance covered by those boys was ten miles: they reminded us of the Children of Hamelin who followed the magic notes of the piper.

This example of the draw of the pipes, confirmed in Colonel Mulholland's mind the importance of the L.I.R having its own Pipe Band once again.

70 Years as Colonel!

Within weeks of bidding the Regiment bon voyage for Ulster, Field Marshal the Duke of Connaught was back reviewing the London Irish Rifles as part of the celebrations to mark his sixtieth year as the Regiment's Honorary Colonel. It was a very large parade, described[7] on the Pathé Newsreel of the day as "a celebration for a grand old soldier".

Prince Arthur, the Duke of Connaught was a son of Queen Victoria. From his acceptance of the role of Honorary Colonel in 1871 he had always kept in touch with the Regiment, often leading it at the annual review.

The Duke was to remain the Regiment's Honorary Colonel until his death in 1942. P/M Franklin of the London Rifles was in a band, formed entirely of Pipe Majors, who played at the Duke's State funeral.

The Duke of Connaught inspects the Regimental Pipers of the London Irish Rifles in 1931, on the occasion of the 60th Anniversary of his appointment as Honorary Colonel of the Regiment.

The aptly named steam engine 'The London Irish Rifleman' took the L.I.R. from Euston to Fleetwood for the ferry to Belfast.

Tim McCarthy, Italy, 1987. One of eight Second World War London Irish Band members with links to the Dagenham Town Irish Pipe Band - a band originally formed when the Ford Motor Co. moved its production from Cork to Dagenham in 1931.

The Demise of the Military Band of the London Irish Rifles

During his time as Commanding Officer, Colonel Mulholland had great difficulty getting the Regimental Military Band to parade. In his opinion[8] it was "a brass band of hired assassins who would only parade if they had no other [private] engagement". So when the War Office instructed (circa 1930) that regimental bands should change the pitch of their instruments, Colonel Mullholland decided to stand down the L.I.R. Regimental Band rather than totally re-equip them with the new musical instruments so required. Remembering the uplifting effect of the First World War pipe bands, he had decided that the funds would be better used to establish a self contained Pipe Band in place of the Regimental Band.

A full size pipe band of Territorial soldiers did not happen overnight as there were a number of obstacles to be surmounted. However there was a considerable supply of pipers and drummers versed in the Irish tradition available from the proliferation of civilian 'Irish' bands in London. What is obvious from the 1931 'Operation Ulster' photographs is that the Regiment's 'official' pipers and drummers were augmented by many civilian guest musicians so as to put on a good show.

Irish Bands in London

The first Irish pipe band in London had been the Borough Pipe Band. This was founded in 1892 and was still performing in 2003. This was followed by several Boys Brigade pipe bands including the Haverstock Hill Catholic Boys Brigade which contributed a significant number of pipers and drummers to the L.I.R. 2nd. Bn.'s First World War Bands (see pages 19). By the 1920's the Canning Town Brian Boru Pipe Band, Tottenham Irish Pipe Band, and the Great Western Railway Pipe Band were active in London. The 1930's saw the ascendancy of the Dagenham Town Irish Pipe Band, to an extent at the expense of the Tottenham Band.

Furthermore many Catholic Churches in pre-war London had drum and fife bands which understandably had extensive Irish repertoires. Amongst such bands were the East End bands of St. Patrick's (Wapping), Our Lady Immaculate (Limehouse), St. Mary & St. Michael's (Stepney) and St. Anne's (Custom House) There were also church bands at Hoxton, Bethnal Green, Dockhead, Downham and Deptford.

The post Second World War era saw the emergence of the Tower Hill Pipe Band, the Deptford Irish Pipe Band and the South London Girl Pipers. The new millennium has seen the emergence of the Castle Pipers.

Migration between bands was not uncommon and during its one hundred years existence the Pipes and Drums of the London Irish Rifles has had in its ranks musicians who had played in one or more of the above civilian bands. Two civilian London pipe bands in particular had a major long term impact on the Pipes & Drums of the London Irish Rifles.

In 1931 the Ford Motor Company closed its works in Cork, Eire, as it centralised its production at the newly built facility in Dagenham, London. In the transferred Irish workforce were pipers and drummers from the legendary Cork Volunteer Pipe Band. These musicians immediately formed the Dagenham Town Irish Pipe Band and rekindled in the East End the flames first ignited by the defunct Canning Town Brian Boru Pipe Band (see page 19). The Second World

War Pipes & Drums of the London Irish Rifles had at least eight members with links with the Dagenham Band. These were Tim McCarthy (see page 29), Allan Nicholson (see page 104) and most noteworthy Eddie, Toddy and Jack Shanahan (see page 106), Pat O'Brien (see page 71), Sandy O'Callaghan (see page 36) and George Willis (see page 113) all of whom had attended St. Mary's & St. Joseph's R.C. School in Poplar.

Also during the inter-war years, but across in West London, the Great Western Railwaymen's Pipe Band was operational. Its Pipe Major was a Con Clancey who had been in the L.I.R. Band and so, whilst the Railwaymen's Pipe Band was ostensibly Scottish and wore the MacKenzie tartan, its repertoire was not lacking in L.I.R tunes. Notable pipers schooled at this band were Johnny Franklin (see page 75) and Archie Evans (see page 65); respectively the Pipe Majors of 1st. and 2nd. Bn.'s Bands during the Second World War.

Towards a Credible and Viable Pipe Band

The foundations of the revived Pipes & Drums were laid by Col. Mulholland but it was not until the arrival of Captain Jack Macnamara and the later appointment of Johnny Franklin as Pipe Major, that the Regiment had in place the necessary organising charisma and piping skills to sustain a credible and viable Pipe Band.

Lt.-Col. Jack Macnamara MP

Born in 1905, it was[9] as a young subaltern that Jack Macnamara joined the L.I.R in 1934 after regular army service with the Royal Fusiliers. From the start his "enthusiasm and comradeship with all ranks helped to put new zest and energy into the Regiment". He recognised "the dangers that would befall an unarmed Britain and did all within his power to revive public and official interest in the Territorial Army".

In modern day management parlance Jack Macnamara had a vision of what was needed for the Country, the Regiment, and in the context of this book, how a regimental pipe band could assist in the achievement of these objectives.

His rise in the Regiment and in public life was meteoric. Apart from being heavily involved in military matters, his concern for the future of Britain had taken him into politics. After unsuccessfully contesting the parliamentary constituency of West Ham, he was elected Chelmsford's M.P. in 1936.

By the time he was officially appointed the C.O. of the London Irish Rifles in 1938, he had been instrumental in the Regiment emphasising its 'Irishness' by:

- becoming a Territorial Bn. of the R.U.R.;
- publicising itself as a part of the Territorial Army;
- adopting the caubeen for all ranks (see page 122);
- acquiring highly decorative pipe banners;
- the carrying of shillelaghs by officers.

Lt.-Col. Jack Macnamara M.P.
A first rate communicator and motivator who, like chieftains of old, understood the military value of the Pipes & Drums.

Macnamara's Band, 1938, in new dress uniforms and with new pipe ribbons and banners flying. In the front rank is Pipe Cpl. Woods, a veteran of the 1st. Bn.'s First World War Band.

Regrettably Lt.-Col. Macnamara never achieved his ambition to lead 'his' Regiment into action. He was promoted to a command in the newly formed R.A.F Regiment in February 1942 (i.e. before the L.I.R. left the United Kingdom for the war).

It is poetic, however, that he was killed in December 1944 whilst paying a visit to the 1st. Bn. of the London Irish Rifles during its campaign at the Senio River, Italy. It was reported[10] that:

> the London Irish were taking over positions from a Gurkha Regiment and as the men moved up into the lines, Colonel Macnamara recognised many old faces. The desire to see 'his' men in action was overwhelming and he went to see the forward Companies. It was while he was with 'C' Company that he was caught in a sudden mortar bombardment and killed.

Colonel Macnamara was initially buried at the front, but Pipe Major John Franklin subsequently arranged a trio of pipers to be withdrawn from their forward positions to pipe 'their' Colonel to his final resting place (see photograph on page 137). He was buried in Forli War Cemetry, Italy, next to Rifleman 'Tiny' Staines, a member of the Band's stretcher bearing platoon.

Pipe Major Johnny Franklin B.E.M.

It was in 1928 that Johnny Franklin joined the L.I.R. as a company piper. By 1937 he had been appointed Pipe Major. He was involved with the Band for nearly 60 years and in a chronological history such as this book he could feature in almost ever chapter. However a composite appreciation of his contribution is summarised in that part of this book that describes his greatest honour, and arguably the Band's greatest day (see page 75).

The Gathering Storm

Returning to April 1939, when the order came to double the strength of the Territorial Forces, Lt.-Col. Macnamara had been ready for some time. Consequently the London Irish became one of the first units to reach full strength and then to complete its second line. It was later said[11] "The Pipe Band played a leading part [in 1939] in helping to form the 2nd. Bn. so quickly".

By the summer of 1939 the intense military preparation of the 1st. and 2nd. Battalions had commenced in the spare time of this volunteer part time Regiment. At the same time the enlarged Band was undergoing training to harmonise the piping and drumming styles of those pipers, drummers and musicians who had recently volunteered from civilian bands to augment the peacetime Band. Despite holding full time jobs the men of the London Irish Rifles approached their military and musical training with vigour and enthusiasm.

On the evening of 31 August 1939, Lt. Col. Macnamara wrote[12] in his diary that:

> We had the order to mobilise. It was broadcast by the BBC on the wireless at 4 p.m. Men in uniform started coming in almost at once. They passed the doctor, signed various forms and drew their arms and ammunition. By 10.30 p.m. our Battalion was almost complete except for men away from London.
>
> At about half hourly intervals the companies marched off to their war stations. Each company went a little way with the Band playing the Wearing of the Green and the Minstrel Boy - the first party had a great ovation from the crowd.

The Regiment (and the Band) Jack Macnamara had rejuvenated was ready!

References:

1. *The Story of the London Irish Rifles* edited Major R Cockburn M.B.E,
        published 1984 by the London Irish Rifles Regimental Association; page 33.
2. *The London Irish at War* published by The Regimental Association London Irish, 1949.
3. *The Emerald* No.15; The L.I.R. Invade Ulster by Col. J.A. Mulholland.
4. op. cit. Col. J.A .Mulholland.
5. *The Regimental Centenary* published by the London Irish Rifles Regimental Association, 1959; page 63.
6. op. cit. Col. J.A. Mulholland.
7. www.britishpathe.com/product_display.php?searchfilm=london+irish+rifles&Search.x=29&Search.y=24
8. op. cit. *The Regimental Centenary*; page 60.
9. op. cit. *The London Irish at War*; page 17. repeatedly includes the spelling of the C.O.'s name as 'Macnamara' as do other immediate post war sources.
10. op cit. *The London Irish at War*; page 19.
11. *The Emerald* No.27; Brigadier C.R.Briten; page 7.
12. *The Emerald* No.32; page 28.

The Second World War (1939-45)

The Wartime Bands of the London Irish Rifles.
The Massed Pipes and Drums of the First, Second and the Young Soldiers' Battalions.

It is impossible to do justice in this book to all the action seen by the London Irish Rifles during the Second World War. Fortunately it has been comprehensively recorded[1] in *The London Irish at War*. That book recounts the Regiment's actions that yielded a further 40 battle honours – a number not exceeded in that conflict by any Regiment in the British Army.

This chapter focuses on the hundred or so drummers, buglers and pipers who played in one of the L.I.R. Bands during the Second World War.

Immediately on the outbreak of war, the War Office somewhat unimaginatively decreed[2] that, to ensure that "the horrors of war should be officially plumbed to their drabbest depths, there should be no more British military bands". There was to be no government funding for what nowadays would be termed 'triumphalist' military music and to this end all band funds were frozen.

After nine months of protests, and the vociferous demands of the Press and the B.B.C., the War Office authorised the formation and funding of one Band per Regiment. This restoration of military music was academic to the L.I.R. whose Pipes and Drums had continued to perform anyway.

As already indicated in the previous chapter, by the summer of 1939, the London Irish Rifles comprised of two Battalions, each with its own Pipe Band. Later a Young Soldiers Battalion was raised and this too had a Pipe Band. Apart from the 1941 War Weapons Week in London (see page 43) these Bands never played together and their paths seldom crossed. So, for the remainder of this chapter the story of each Band is told separately.

The Day War broke out

In the summer of 1939 the 1st. Battalion London Irish Rifles had been assigned to the 1st. London Infantry Division. In the likelihood of war, this Division's responsibility was to assist the Metropolitan Police: the London Irish Rifles being detailed to support the Police at Brixton, South London.

On the morning of 3 September 1939, the 1st. Battalion marched, with its pipes and drums playing, from Brixton Police Station to the Parish Church for a service. Whilst the men were at prayer, the C.O. received a message telling him that war had been declared. An announcement was made and the service ended with special prayers.

As the Band led the parade back to the Police Station the eerie solemn silence throughout Brixton (and one would guess London and the Country) was shattered by air raid sirens being continuously sounded. It was thought that this would be followed by the drone of enemy aircraft and then the sound of bombs and machine guns. But it did not happen. It was later discovered that the sirens had been sounded as a snap test of the civil defences.

Ashdown Forest (late 1939 - early 1940)

The 1st. Battalion's 'esprit de corps', that was to see it through the six years of war, was consolidated during the winter of 1939-40 in Sussex. Initially there were a lot of comings and goings, both for the 1st. Battalion and its Band. As individuals' talents were recognised and appropriate duties assigned, many transferred to specialist activities and regiments. But all the time fresh recruits soon filled these gaps.

By the late spring of 1940, the Battalion had undergone extensive training; roles and responsibilities were well understood and with the addition of 'L' Company (who had been young soldiers trained at Bognor) the 1st. Bn. and its Band were back to strength.

Sunday Church Parade was a regular duty for all London Irish Pipe Bands. Here the 1st. Bn. parade at Danes Hill near Ashdown Forest, November 1939.

Piper Macnamara

Like chieftains of old, Lt.-Col. Macnamara regarded the Band as his personal retinue. There were those who would argue that as a consequence the Band tended to have an easy life. Certainly the C.O's secretary, two batmen, a bodyguard/driver, as well as the regimental post corporal, tailor and band storeman were all drawn from the Band.

The special relationship between the C.O. and his Band was cultivated (some would say exploited) by the bandsmen. A story has been anonymously provided concerning the first Christmas of the War:

> The piper who was the secretary to the C.O. had used his good offices (if not the C.O.'s signature) to obtain a firkin [a 72 pint barrel] of beer for the Band's Christmas festivities.
>
> On Christmas Day, after a dinner of chicken passing itself off as turkey, followed by something resembling plum duff, the Band retired to its hut to commence its liquid celebration. To legitimise the ceilidh, the C.O. had been invited as the guest of honour. It fact he was the only guest!
>
> Once Lt.-Col. Macnamara had arrived and was safely ensconced with a glass of illicit beer in his hand, a notice was affixed to the exterior of the door to the effect:

NO ADMITTANCE - C.O.'S PRIVATE FUNCTION

To ensure gatecrashers who chose to ignore the notice, couldn't gain entry, the door was bolted. The shindig began. Beer was drunk; songs were sung; pipes were played. A good time was being had by all and the C.O. was encouraged to display his piping skills, which he had developed with the help of his secretary.

Jack (all pretentious formality being lost after the third pint) gave the Band his rendition of 'Cock of the North' and almost brought the hut down with 'Garryowen'. As a mark of the band's appreciation, the C.O. was presented with the piper's insignia that is traditionally worn of the right lower arm. Everybody present, including the C.O., played 'Garryowen' again.

Lt-Colonel Macnamara with Piper O'Callaghan & Bugler Mullins,1940.

(photograph from R.G.Harris' *The Irish Regiments* 1693-1999 published by Spellmount Ltd and reproduced with permission.)

The rest of the camp now definitely knew that the Band were up to something again. The R.S.M. went to investigate. If the notice on the door was provocation, the bolted entrance was like a red rag to a bull. He rushed to the nearest fire point, grabbed an axe, returned to the Band's hut and made light work of smashing his way in. His elation was short lived! As his adrenaline levels dropped and the room came into focus the first face he saw was his C.O., who appeared to be saying:

> "I trust Santa has put enough new pennies in your stocking for you to make good the damage you've just inflicted on the King's property."

They say that every dog has its day, and the R.S.M. did not have to wait long. At parade the next morning Lt. Colonel Macnamara was already wearing the piper's insignia on his uniform. The R.S.M. couldn't believe his luck in finding his C.O. improperly dressed.

In a stage whisper he advised the C.O. that he appeared to have a deposit on his arm, and that he should quickly remove it for fear of appearing improperly dressed.

Honour was satisfied, and the smashed door and the piper's insignia became mere figments of the imagination.

The 'Phoney War' gave rise to staged photographs.
Here the men of the London Irish Rifles, complete with pipers, defend the beaches of Kent in 1940.

The Band's Involvement in the Evacuation of Dunkirk

Whilst the Territorial Regiments were being brought up to speed during that period known as the 'Phoney War' (September 1939 to May 1940), thirteen divisions[3] of the Regular British Army and their Allies were in mainland Europe. They were desperately fighting to stop the German advance. However the strength of the German forces had been seriously underestimated in terms of their equipment, transport and fire power. The Allies' situation was rapidly deteriorating. Hitler's armies continued to sweep west through Holland, Belgium and France towards the British Isles.

At short notice the 1st. Bn. London Irish Rifles was moved to Kent to defend the Isle of Thanet against invasion. By early May nearly all of the escape routes from Europe to the Channel had been cut off and the Allies found themselves being funnelled towards the beaches of Dunkirk.

May 10th saw Winston Churchill replace Neville Chamberlain as the British Prime Minister. On the 14th May 1940 the BBC made the following announcement[4]:

> The Admiralty have made an Order requesting all owners of self-propelled pleasure craft between 30 and 100 feet in length to send particulars to the Admiralty within 14 days from today if they have not already been offered or requisitioned.

On the 26th May 1940 the War Office ordered the immediate evacuation of the troops trapped in the vicinity of Dunkirk. The next day an armada of 693 ships (including 39 Destroyers, 36 Minesweepers, 77 trawlers, 26 Yachts and a variety of other small and not so small craft) was assembled along the Kent coast and 'Operation Dynamo' began. The evacuation had already become a race against time as Belgium had sued for peace the previous day and the Luftwaffe was blitzing the harbour of Dunkirk out of use.

The intended role for the London Irish in 'Operation Dynamo' was to guard the piers at Ramsgate and Margate and to help the evacuees ashore. However the first wave of boats to return from Dunkirk had clearly suffered heavily from aerial attack and the Royal Navy asked the L.I.R. to set up and operate anti-aircraft positions on some of the larger civilian craft for the remainder of the evacuation. The vessels selected were not unknown to the Londoners, as the *Queen of Thanet*, the *Royal Sovereign* and the *Duchess of Fife* were all well known Thames pleasure steamers in peace time.

The Band provide an ack-ack team for the Royal Sovereign which included Piper Pat O'Brien, who later was to become the Band's Pipe Major and did so much to preserve the Band in the latter half of the 20th Century (see page 71). The *Royal Sovereign* made sixteen trips to Dunkirk and brought back an estimated 16,000 troops. By 4 June 1940, when the operation came to an end, 198,000 British and 140,000 French and Belgian troops had been evacuated in total. The men who were saved represented a considerable part of the experienced troops possessed by Great Britain and were an inestimable gain to the Allies.

The task of the Band was not however finished. For the next month, they piped to their graves a considerable number of British and Allied soldiers who died in hospital after reaching sanctuary from Dunkirk.

Piper 'F' meets Monty

Sidney George Newcombe was the archetypal South Londoner who had a way with words - well one word actually! He unrelentingly used the 'F' word and its variants as a noun, verb, adjective, adverb, superlative, and some times even as an expletive. Within months of the joining the L.I.R. in 1934, he had been christened Piper 'F' by Father Devas, the R.C. Padre. The name was to stick.

'F' was without doubt a very fine musician capable of playing the piccolo, clarinet, drum, and was a bugler of the highest quality. As a Welsh Guards Bandsman, he was one of the eight buglers who sounded the Last Post and Reveille in 1920 when the permanent stone Cenotaph (see page 25) was unveiled in Whitehall and the Unknown Warrior was laid to rest in Westminster Abbey.

He was the first to admit[5] his "piping left a lot to be desired", and as to his marching whilst playing the pipes it was said[6] "his left foot had a guardsman step and his right one a rifleman's". It was no coincidence that he was located in the back rank of the pipers.

On mobilisation, 'F' was made the Post Corporal for the 1st. Battalion and soon became universally recognised as a unique character. His sense of fun and humour was obvious to all, and his inventiveness and quick wit soon became legendary. An officer[7] was to comment "his appreciation of a situation had to be heard to be believed. Piper 'F' was a man of immense resourcefulness; he could produce smoked salmon in the middle of Timbuctoo or a grass skirt in Greenland. He was

General Montgomery
inspects 1st. Bn. L.I.R. accompanied by its C.O. Lt.Col. Jack Macnamara, Kent, 1940.

no respecter of rank or office but he endeared himself to all by his unorthodoxy."

In 1941, in his late thirties with decades of army service behind him, Piper 'F' was both literally and metaphorically an old soldier, with a sharp London edge. He was a combination of the best (or worst) characteristics of Sgt. Ernie Bilko and Arthur Daley, the last man an officer would want the Regiment to be judged by, so one can imagine the anguish amongst the officers on a summer's day in Kent 1941 as the following scene unfolds.

A Ceremonial Parade and Inspection by General Montgomery (later Field Marshal Viscount Montgomery) had been arranged to boost the morale of the 1st. Battalion. All was going to plan until Murphy's Law kicked in. During the inspection, the General progressed along the drawn up ranks of riflemen in what might be called a cursory manor but on inspecting the Band stopped stone dead in front of Piper 'F'. To a man the Battalion held its breath. The General looked long and hard at 'F' and asked[8]:

"What part of Ireland do you come from?"

Quick as a flash, but in his normal Cockney accent 'F' replied:

"County Camberwell, Sir."

The response at the time is not recorded, but in a subsequent letter[9] to Lieutenant Colonel Macnamara, the General described the Battalion as

" ...splendid. The men have the light of battle in their eyes ...... if every battalion in the Army was like them we should do well."

Irish Dancing as Physical Training

While at Lydd, Kent, the 1st. Battalion's Commanding Officer decided that physical training should take the form of Irish Dancing. The men were to be introduced to the joys of the four hand reel – a set dance the Pipes & Drums had long enjoyed in moments of relaxation. Come the appointed morning the Band gave a demonstration. Then the entire Battalion, in P.T. kit and army boots, tried to imitate the steps as two pipers played the 'Rakes of Mallow'.

Every morning for the next two weeks this aerobic physical training continued. In the end, the experiment was discontinued at the Medical Officer's insistence. Too many men were reporting for sick parade with either bruised shins accidentally inflicted by army boots, or more intentional physical damage, sustained in debates between riflemen as to the sequence of steps and the finesse required.

The Band at Haverhill (1941-2) and its Return 35 years later

The 1st. Battalion had mixed memories of its time in Haverhill. All can remember being assigned to two months of back breaking work bringing in the sugar-beet harvest for the farmers whose labour had been conscripted. Some remember discrimination by the locals on the account of being both Londoners and Irish. In fact the Battalion, led by its Pipes and Drums, was turned away from the first Suffolk church service it tried to attend. The next Sunday, alternative arrangements were made but the route to the second (and welcoming) church was always past the first church with the entire Battalion participating as the Band played 'Killaloe' (see page 142).

However the predominating memories of the last town the Battalion was billeted in before being sent overseas, are all happy and are best summed up by the following report[10] of the Band's return 35 years later:

> The visit to Haverhill was more than just a pleasant job way out in the country. It was a sentimental journey to a town in which the 1st. Battalion of the London Irish Rifles spent many happy weeks before going overseas. It was such a happy place that more than thirty members married local girls and many of them settled in the area after the War.
>
> That memories run very deep was shown by a woman who was shopping when the Band played past the store she was in. The woman put her shopping basket down very quickly and ran out of the store and fell in behind the band, saying that she remembered marching with the band to the special Christmas party organised by the 1st. Battalion when she was six years old. A man in the crowd said that when he was sixteen, and a member of the Home Guard, he always marched every Sunday with the local Company behind the London Irish Pipe Band on their way to Church. This was done at the personal invitation of Lt. Colonel Macnamara, the Commanding Officer.
>
> The Band, in good strength of eighteen pipers and ten drummers gave a tremendous show and caused much admiration as they played through the streets. The cheering and the pleasure they gave seemed to inspire them, it was a great day.
>
> After the show the Band were entertained regally in an ex-service men's club, with a first class buffet and ample beer. The band was called upon later in the evening to put on a special show; a kind of cabaret turn...................."

Unbeknown to the 1977 Band, such a 'cabaret turn' was a feature of the 'All Ranks Dance (officers' attendance compulsory)' that the 1st. Bn. held every Saturday night whilst at Haverhill during the Second World War. As recalled[11] some 60 years later by the daughter of the late Col. Richards, the culmination of the Band's performances in 1942 was, "to march round the perimeter of the dance floor to be followed by all those present".

From Dance Band to Second Battalion Pipe Band

During the 1930's the Jack Hylton Orchestra was the most famous dance band in Europe. Apart from regularly performing throughout the U.K., the Band[12] toured Europe sixteen times. At one stage it also had a series of thirteen one hour radio show in the U.S.A. – the first of which was a mid-Atlantic broadcast from the liner taking them to the States. In 1940, Jack Hylton decided to disband his Orchestra, as so many of his seasoned performers had left to serve in the army as military musicians. Two such musicians were Pipers Lehmann and Beck who had joined the 2nd. Bn. Pipe Band at the start of the war. Former members of the reed section of the Hylton Orchestra, they soon adjusted to the pipes. Mick Lehmann was particularly proficient and he was rapidly promoted to Pipe Corporal. As such he was instrumental in extending the Band's repertoire.

When the Band led the Regiment through Chichester, it played 'Sussex by the

**The 1941 Pipe Band
of the 2nd. Bn. L.I.R.**
included members of the reed
section of the world-renowned Jack
Hylton Orchestra.

Sea' – much to the delight of the locals. During a four day's forced march from St. Albans to Lowestoft, Mick eased the boredom by sprinkling the 'Top Ten' of the day amongst the usual Irish repertoire he was expected to play as he marched with the H.Q. Company.

However his lasting contribution to the mythology of the London Irish Rifles was the occasion when he deputised for P/M Archie Evans in providing the music for the changing of the H.Q. guard. As the incoming guard marched from the distance towards the sergeant acting as the guard commander, the strains (if not the words) of 'you are my sunshine, my only sunshine, you make me happy when skies are grey ....' could be heard. It is alleged that the incoming guard sashayed rather than marched towards its duties.

Reveille at Midnight

There was a young Welsh bugler in the 2nd. Battalion's Band called 'Taffy' Edwards who was a non drinking, early to bed, God fearing man of the Valleys. The worst swear word he uttered under extreme provocation was 'Pesky'. It is remembered[13] that, while stationed at Haverford West, the remainder of his hut just made it back before lights out – needless to say they had been drinking. They decided to wake Taffy up at 23.59 and tell him to blow 'Reveille'. It was only after he had played the first couple of notes that the rest of the hut managed to subdue him (and his bugle) before too much damage was done.

41

The Young Soldiers Battalion

Apart from its 1st. and 2nd. Bns., for a short period, the Regiment also had a Young Soldiers Battalion – the 70th London Irish Rifles. This was formed early in 1940 and was for young men between the ages of eighteen and nineteen-and-a-half. The object was to train them to the highest standards of drill, skill-at-arms, discipline, and turn-out, so that when they became of operational military age (which at that time was twenty) they would be fit to take their places as soldiers in the 1st. and 2nd. Battalions. Drafts of well-trained young men were frequently dispatched to the senior battalions. Apart from undergoing training, senior platoons of the Young Soldiers Battalion also took over guard duties at vulnerable points at factories and other important installations in north west London.

The Young Soldiers Battalion followed the London Irish tradition and had its own Pipe Band, who were trained by pipers and drummers transferred from the 1st. Bn.'s Band. In time many of these young musicians transferred to other bands including both the 1st. and 2nd. Bn.'s Pipe Bands.

The 70th Battalion ceased to exist in January 1943, when the War Office revised operational military age down to eighteen years old. Consequently all such Young Soldiers Battalions were disbanded and their personnel sent to senior units. In the case of the L.I.R. Young Soldiers were predominantly assigned to the 70th Bn. Royal Ulster Rifles.

Too young to fight .....
.... but getting ready!
The Young Soldiers of the London Irish Rifles were a Battalion in miniature, including its own Pipe Band. On reaching operational military age, the young soldiers were transferred to senior units.

Almost Altogether

The Bands of the 1st. Battalion, the 2nd. Battalion and the 70th Young Soldiers Battalion only played together once during their separate wartime existences. That was during War Weapons Week 1941. For that week, the Massed Pipes & Drums of the London Irish Rifles comprised of five ranks of eight pipers per rank, a twenty two piece drum section, three bugle majors and Tara, the Regimental Mascot (see page 117). Truly a monumentally large Pipe Band!

After playing 'Kelly' and 'O'Donnell a Bhu' at the start of the main parade that week, the Senior Pipe Major, Johnny Franklin said the next tunes were to be 'Kelly' and 'O'Donnell a Bhu'. The pipers nearest Johnny pointed out that these tunes had only just been played, so the P/M said that the next tunes would be 'the Wearing of the Green' and 'the Minstrel Boy'. Bert Thackery, the Senior Bugle Major out in front of the Band then gave the order to play. Those nearest the Pipe Major, who had been party to the discussion and corrected instruction, struck up 'the Wearing of the Green' and 'the Minstrel Boy'. Those pipers further away, and oblivious to the change, executed the last order they had heard and played 'Kelly' and 'O'Donnell a Bhu' again.

Everyone knew that the parade was being covered by a BBC outside broadcasting unit and the Band were hopeful that they would hear themselves on the six o'clock Radio News.

So after the parade, all three Bands rushed back to Wembley where they were stationed for the week, and gathered round an accumulator powered wireless just in time to hear the news reader introduce a recording of the Massed Bands of the London Irish Rifles. He went on to draw the attention of his listeners to the Band playing, as only an Irish Pipe Band could, two different melodies at the same time!

The Only Time Together.
The Pipes and Drums of all three Battalion of the London Irish Rifles come together for the first and only time to play for the 1941 War Weapons Week.

First Battalion Embark for Egypt but arrive in Iraq

In August 1942 the 1st. Battalion set sail for Egypt in the extreme discomfort of the H.M.T *Orduna*. This ship had been built as a passenger liner in 1914. However by the time the 1st. Battalion of the London Irish Rifles boarded her, she was a cargo carrier converted into a troop carrier. All reports[14] agree the conditions were dire "with little water, little ventilation, poor food, no extra amenities".

After a month at sea (with no shore leave allowed during refuelling at Freetown) the Battalion arrived at Cape Town and were ashore for about a week. A Band member at the time remembers[15]:

Mickey Nolan had a relation in the local Christian Brothers' College and we all went to visit him. Our Band played for the College's Pipe Band. This Band was directly supported by the South African Army who supplied reeds and music. In return the Army had a ready supply of good pipers when the pupils were eligible for national service.

The Brothers asked for two of our blue plumes to place at the feet of the statues of St. Anthony and St. Christopher. They said they would pray for the Regiment's success and that the Band would return safely one day to collect the plumes.

One of our number that day was Billy Tracey, a very young bugler, who was later to accidentally drown in the Tigris at Kirkuk, Iraq. We later learned the College's Band had adopted a bugle tune we had shown them and named it 'Tracey' after learning of Billy's death.

During the shore leave the Pipes and Drums led a parade through the streets and the South Africans took to their hearts the men in the caubeens. They gave the troops a great reception and their generosity was almost overwhelming.

(ABOVE LEFT)
H.M. King George VI
bids the 1st. Bn. L.I.R *bon voyage* and good luck, July 1942.

(ABOVE RIGHT)
R.M.Ss. *Orduna* (ABOVE) and *The Duchess of York* (BELOW) photographed before they were converted to troop carriers.

It was whilst in Cape Town that the Battalion learnt it was to go to Iraq. The purpose was to guard not only the oil installations against attack by saboteurs and parachutists but also the many large dumps of ammunitions the Allies had placed in the hills for use against the Germans should they break through the Russian defences in the Caucasus.

Second Battalion Embarks for the Unknown

On 10 November 1942, the 2nd. Battalion boarded H.M.T. *Duchess of York* at Glasgow. This ship, originally built for the Canadian Pacific Railway Company in 1929, was now part of a vast convoy of troop ships, with Royal Navy escorts, heading for an unknown destination. However before even leaving the Clyde, the cat was out of the bag! News was received of the Allied landings in North Africa and everybody now had a very good idea of where they were going.

But before they arrived, the 2nd. Battalion had to survive what was soon dubbed 'the Drunken Duchess'. The men not only had to endure the wild staggering of the Duchess herself, but also the unique oscillating motion she induced in the hammocks as they 'slept' in the night. As the pipes were stowed away, there was no music to break the boredom. The only entertainment was endless games of Bingo.

After twelve long days and nights aboard the Duchess, the London Irish Rifles arrived in North Africa[16] and "with the bagpipes leading, the 2nd. Battalion went safely ashore in full marching order."

The voyage was officially described as without incident. The *Duchess of York* was not to be so lucky nine months later. She was sunk by a Luftwaffe bomb on 11 July 1943 whilst making a similar troop carrying run. Some 90 lives were lost.

The Irish Brigade in North Africa (1942-3)

Together with the 6th.Royal Inniskilling Fusiliers, and the 1st. Royal Irish Fusiliers, the 2nd. Bn. London Irish Rifles constituted the Irish Brigade. In North Africa this Brigade was to be part of the British First Army – an Army tasked with taking Tunis from the German and Italian forces.

Within weeks of landing[17], the London Irish Rifles were in the line. The valley of Bou Arada and its hills were to be the home of the L.I.R. for the first two months of 1943. They suffered heavily in their January attacks and had borne the brunt of the German's counter offensive in February. In the encounters of Bou Arada the London Irish distinguished themselves but at "..... crippling costs". sustaining "grievous losses ....and cruel casualties". Bou Arada was to be the 2nd. Battalion's (and the Regiment's) first of many Second World War battle honours.

Late March saw the 2nd. Battalion, London Irish Rifles withdrawn to a rest area and its severely depleted numbers augmented by a large draft of officers and men - mostly from the 70th Bn. the Royal Ulster Rifles, many of whom had started the war with the 70th Bn. (Young Soldiers) London Irish Rifles.

The final push towards Tunis started with a concerted effort to clear the enemy from its heavily fortified mountain positions to the south of Tunis – called by some the 'Siegfried Line of Tunisia'.

The offensive commenced in early April, and by the end of the month, and having gained several more battle honours, the London Irish were "looking down majestically on to the Medjez Plain and Tunis beyond". By 7th May the armour of

the First Army had secured the outskirts of Tunis and the L.I.R. were sent to clear up the docks. Fortunately the enemy had no fight left in them and Italians and Germans streamed out in their thousands to surrender. "The people of Tunis went mad with delight at their deliverance."

First Victory Parade.
Tunisians hear the Pipes & Drums of the 2nd. Battalion of the London Irish Rifles in May 1943.

The Invasion of Sicily (1943)

July 1943 and the invasion of Sicily saw[18] the Allies setting foot on continental Europe for the first time in over three years. Both Battalions of the London Irish Rifles were involved.

After an inactive year in Iraq guarding sand (and the oil beneath it), the 1st. Bn.'s first Sicilian job was to mop up behind the first wave of allied troops who had landed three days before them. This was done smoothly; prisoners were taken and there were no casualties. All this changed however when the 1st. Bn. took part in a large scale, night-time operation at Fosso Bottacetto. The German positions were fortified with pill boxes and earth works and although the L.I.R achieved its objective, others in the line did not and a general withdrawal was ordered. The attack had literally been a baptism of fire for the 1st. Bn. and many were killed or wounded.

Meanwhile, on the 1st August, the 2nd. Battalion was given the task of taking three hills behind Centuripe, a village perched on the top of a formidable line of steep hills which was regarded as the key position in the German defence line across Sicily. After two of the three hills were quickly taken the plan was revised and the London Irish Rifles joined the Irish Brigade in the main attack on Centuripe. Just before dawn on 3rd August the village fell but there was no respite. The Salso and Simeto Rivers now had to be crossed in the push northwards. Fierce fighting was experienced at both locations, resulting in more battle honours for the 2nd. Bn. After the rivers, the Irish faced more hills. Victory at Monte Maletto left the Irish Brigade half way along the western slopes of Mount Etna – some two thousand feet above sea level.

On the eastern side of Etna, the 1st. Bn. the London Irish Rifles (as part of the 168 Brigade) was now pushing the Germans northwards to the sea, in what was to be known as the 'Pursuit to Messina' – the 1st. Bn.'s first battle honour of the Second World War.

Summer 1943
From the flat, sunny climes of **Iraq** (TOP RIGHT) to the wet mountain of **Sicily** (BELOW LEFT).

General Montgomery
(BELOW RIGHT) motivates the 1st. Battalion L.I.R. in Egypt before it leaves for Sicily.

Victory in Sicily

On 18th August General Montgomery announced:

> The campaign in Sicily is over .... the Germans have been driven
> out and ...... the Allies are in possession of the whole island.

A Brief Respite

After continuous action for six weeks with little sleep, both Battalions of the London Irish Rifles enjoyed some well earned R&R – the 2nd. Battalion by the Mediterranean Sea, the 1st. Battalion inland at a small town called Piedmont. Here Loos Day was observed[19] with a parade and service. A local composer wrote a tune for the pipes, although the 1st. Battalion's Band was still without most of its instruments, which were in their luggage on a later convoy. This prompted the C.O. to declare that on any future invasion the pipes and drums would be on the first convoy.

The Invasion of Mainland Italy (1943-4)

Although the invasion of mainland Italy started on 3 September 1943, the First and Second Battalions of the London Irish Rifles were not transferred from Sicily until the end of the month. After landing at Salerno, the 1st. Battalion moved inland through mountainous terrain towards Teano. A hundred miles to the east the 2nd. Battalion, having landed at Tarranto, were advancing slowly along the Adriatic coast – the Germans had blown up every bridge and culvert of the main road as they retreated.

During the early winter[20] of 1943-4 the 1st. Bn. saw action at Monte Camino and the Garigliano river, whilst the 2nd. Bn. fought at the Battle of the River Sangro and the taking of Fossacessa.

1944 was the bloodiest year of the Second World War for all in the London Irish Rifles. Its Battalions were sorely depleted by heavy losses at Castelforte, Anzio, the Gustav Line, and the Gothic Line. However the Allied troops inexorably moved northwards. In early 1945, the push towards the River Po accelerated to such an extent that the Allied troops called themselves the Kangaroo Army because they were bounding forward with giant leaps.

To attempt to summarise all the many actions in Italy would be an injustice to both the dead and the survivors. A detailed account is contained in *The London Irish at War* which, although no longer in print, was however available, at the time of writing, for download on the Internet at http://rurmuseum.tripod.com/star.

Stretcher-bearers in Action

Traditionally bandsmen in the British Army have, in time of war, doubled up as stretcher-bearers or 'auxiliary medical personnel' as Article 25 of the 1929 Geneva Convention would call them. The practice in both Battalions of the London Irish Rifles was no different, and many of the Regiment's Band personnel had been trained in front line first aid.

It has been said[21] that the most difficult part of the stretcher-bearers' job came after a major battle when wounded men were in 'no man's land'. Not only did the stretcher bearers witness horrific injuries, they also knew they could not save everyone. However this did not mean they did not try.

The following four contemporaneous reports[22] of L.I.R. stretcher- bearers fearless trying to save their comrades, give a feel of the circumstances in which they operated:

- ... stretcher-bearers moved fearlessly over the ground, tending and evacuating the wounded [after the failed attempt to take the Fosso Bottacetto, Sicily] .... One of them, Piper Tom Brightman, who had been hit in the leg himself moved about calmly and efficiently and tended fifteen wounded men, For these actions Piper Brightman was awarded the Miltary Medal.

- .....[whilst the 1st. Bn. was in Sicily] .. a patrol from 'D' Company was shot at from close range and an officer and two men were killed and several others wounded. One of the latter was badly hurt, and Lance-Cpl. Byrne placed him under cover and returned to Company Headquarters. Here he reported the situation. Two of the company stretcher-bearers, Pipe Cpl. George Willis (see page 113) and Rfn. Staines, then set off, guided by Lance-Cpl. Byrne, to bring back the wounded man. As they approached the spot where he had been hidden, they too, were fired on, and Rfn. Staines was wounded in the arm. The three men continued forward and managed to reach the wounded man. For over half an hour they had to remain under cover, because the slightest movement attracted enemy fire. Eventually, by breaking through a wall and crawling with the laden stretcher, they got the casualty safely back to the L.I.R. lines, a very gallant episode which did not go unrewarded.

- ......the stretcher-bearers of the Battalion again worked splendidly in succouring their wounded comrades. During the occupation of Formelli [near Monte Camino] a signaller of the gunners' observation-post party was wounded while putting down a line on the track leading to the village. Piper George Riley (see page 112) and Rifleman H. Hughes, the stretcher-bearers of 'A' Company, volunteered to bring him in. German machine-guns swept the road and twice they were forced back. Undeterred, they made a third attempt by another route, reached the wounded man, and brought him back to the London Irish lines safely.

- Fine work, too, was done by the Company stretcher-bearers, and another award was the M.M. to Rfn. McDonald, of the Regimental aid-post, for outstanding courage in tending the wounded.

Understandably not all heroics by stretcher-bearers received formal recognition, but those they saved never forgot. Perhaps the most poignant was the case of Sir James Henry ('D' Company Commander 1st. Bn.). He was saved by the prompt actions of Pipe Cpl. Willis who rendered first aid after Sir James was severely wounded by a direct hit on the Company HQ while based on Monte Damiano (Italy 1944). After the War, despite the social gulf between the two men they became good friends. When Sir James died[23] in 1997 the piper who saved his life, those 50 years earlier, played the funeral lament at the family's request.

Piper Tom Brightman M.M.
was awarded the Military Medal in 1943 for tending fifteen wounded men, despite being wounded himself.

The Massive Pipe Band of the Irish Brigade.
St. Patrick's Day Parade, Forli, Italy, 1945.

Piping Interludes

It is the stuff of comic books to suggest that Bands were raising the moral of the men unrelentingly. The truth is that from the Sicilian campaign onwards the pipes and drums were rarely heard. The notable exceptions were on those occasions in 1944-5 when the Battalions were withdrawn from the line for R&R. It is reported[24]:

> When St. Patrick's Day [1945] came, the 2nd. Battalion was out of the line, and a parade was held at Forli. It was notable for a display by the massed pipes and drums of the Irish Brigade, including the Band of the 2nd. Bn. L.I.R. and also the pipes of the 1st. Bn. L.I.R.

The previous year the 1st. Bn. as a whole[25] had not been so lucky.

> On St. Patrick's Day [1944], the 1st Battalion were billeted at Sarno. Through thoughtless staff-work at a high level they were ordered to move that very day to billets farther south. A most successful but delayed observance of the festival was to be subsequently held.

On March 29 the London Irish embarked for Egypt on what was to be their first real rest since before the invasion of Sicily nearly a year before. While staying near Cairo, the London Irish Pipes and Drums represented the Regiment at The London Division's St. George's Day service, playing alongside the London Scottish.

During its time in Egypt The Regimental Band, its pipes, bugles, and drums, under the direction of Pipe-Major Franklin and Bugle-Major Taylor, continued to make an excellent reputation, both in Cairo, where it played at several important ceremonial parades, including that for the King's Birthday and on Empire Day, and at Alexandria, where it played at hospitals, and the racecourse.

By July 1944 the First Battalion's R&R in Egypt[26] was over. As the boat, taking them back to Italy, docked in Taranto harbour:

> ....a strangely familiar sight met the London Irish Rifles as they lined the sides of their ship waiting to disembark. They saw men already ashore wearing the caubeen and hackle. They were the 2nd. Battalion, waiting to go to Egypt. There was only time for a wave and a shout. The ways of the two Battalions parted for many long weary, bitter months, until they took part in the last great race through northern Italy.

On landing, the 1st. Bn. moved to Tivoli, to prepare itself for the final push. While there, the London Irish and the other regiments of the 56th (London) Division were paid a visit by King George VI, the first since he bade them God-speed on the eve of leaving England. Unfortunately no photograph has been found.

Tivoli is not far from Rome. The Eternal City had been captured months earlier and the 1st. Battalion's Band was to contribute to the ancient culture of the city by performing in the Piazza Venezia.

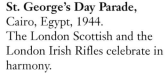

St. George's Day Parade,
Cairo, Egypt, 1944.
The London Scottish and the London Irish Rifles celebrate in harmony.

At different times, whilst in the vicinity of Rome, both the 1st. and 2nd. Battalions of the London Irish Rifles made formal visits to the Pope. The 2nd. Battalion's audience was as part of the now legendary Irish Brigade. It is recorded[27] that:

> a representative party of 150 marched behind their Pipes & Drums up the steps of the Vatican. His Holiness was received by the three pipe majors playing the 'Minstrel Boy'. After a special Mass in St. Peter's, the pipes and drums beat Retreat in the Piazza outside the Basilica.

It is recorded[28] that, during the 1st. Battalion's visit, one enthusiastic officer was so overwhelmed by the occasion that:

> ....he called for three cheers for the Pope. They were given with considerable gusto, to the apparent gratification of His Holiness, but to the evident bewilderment of the Vatican Guard.

Rome 1944.
(ANTI-CLOCKWISE)

Pope Pius XII receives the Irish Brigade.

Brigadier Scott takes the salute as the Irish Brigade march into St. Peter's.

The Pipes & Drums of the 2nd. Bn. London Irish Rifles play in the Piazza Venezia.

Trieste Victory Parade.
The Pipes & Drums of the 1st. Bn.
London Irish Rifles lead the Victory
Parade of the 56th Division.

In August 1944 the 1st. Battalion moved up again into the line for what was to be the long hard slog to gain control of the plains of northern Italy. During the late autumn[29] the Battalion were withdrawn for four days' rest which:

> ....was of great benefit to everybody, and during that period the Battalion met the Irish Regiment of Canada. The respective Bands played to each Battalion, and the Canadians were persuaded to adopt blue hackles in their caubeens. The hackles were conspicuously displayed later in the attack the Canadians made on Coriano, which they captured with great spirit. The hackle has now been permanently adopted by the Canadian Irish.

Italy Surrenders

The month of April 1945 saw both London Irish Battalions in the same military battles and they established direct contact with each other for the first time during the war. After taking the Argenta Gap, they continued to advance over open country towards the River Po; the battle for which was the Regiment's last in the Second World War.

On 2 May 1945 the German Armies in Italy surrendered. Six days later the German High Command surrendered Europe unconditionally and the Flags of Freedom flew[30] all over the continent.

The summer of 1945 was a time of great celebration both at home and abroad. The Pipes & Drums of the London Irish Rifles participated in many parades. The most notable were the 78th Division's Victory Parade near Spittal (Austria) which the 2nd. Bn. attended, and the 56th Division's Parade with the 1st. Bn. at Trieste (near the Italian/Yugoslavian border).

The London Irish P.O.W. Piper

Absent from the Victory Parades in Italy during the Summer of 1945 was Pipe Corporal 7015153 George Willis of the 1st. Bn. Band. Having been captured at Anzio (9th February 1944), he was now Prisoner of War No.278823 at Stalag IVB near Muhlberg just 30 miles north-west of Dresden. The conditions in this camp can be gauged by the following letters from POWs that appeared in the monthly 'Prisoner of War Journal' that the Red Cross and St. John War Organisation published throughout the War.

> There are about 14,000 prisoners[31] of all nationalities at Stalag IVB: the majority of which are British and South African. We sleep in barracks about 200 to a room. Each barrack is long and narrow, about half the floor space being taken up by three tier wooden bunks. The other half accommodates tables and forms. There are two stoves to a barrack........ Outside the hut is a compound slightly larger than a football pitch. There are four other compounds in the camp and we are allowed to walk in any of these.

Another P.O.W. provided[32] a brief summary of a day in Stalag IVB.

> 'Reveille' at 6 a.m.; roll call at 6.30. Brew tea and breakfast (usually a few biscuits or toast). Wash and tidy up and then stroll round the compound while the hut is being swept. The distance right round the two larger compounds together is approximately three quarters of a mile. Drink tea again at 10 o'clock. Weight lifting class 10.30 till 11.30 a.m. German potatoes and vegetables issued next but we keep the spuds and refry them at about 4 o'clock with something from the Red Cross food parcel and have another brew.
>
> At 8 p.m. comes the second roll call, followed by a race to be first back to the barrack for supper, which is usually the same as breakfast. We manage five brews a day from one packet of English tea per week! The time in between is easily filled.

Food Parcels

It was one of the aims of the Red Cross and the Order of St. John of Jerusalem[33] to provide each British and Dominion P.O.W. with a weekly standard food parcel weighing 11 lb (5kg.) including packing. In 1940 it was found necessary to give up the original system of addressing the parcels to individual prisoners. Thereafter they were sent to the International Red Cross Committee at Geneva to be forwarded to the camps in proportion to the number of British P.O.W.s interned in each. They were addressed by the Red Cross to the British Camp Captains for distribution amongst their men. The parcels sent from Great Britain to Geneva were supplemented by consignments from the Dominions, India, the USA, Argentina and Brazil. Clothing (including greatcoats, battledress, underclothing and boots) were packed and dispatched by the British Red Cross.

Relatives and friends could also send parcels but only of tobacco and slab chocolate – though once a quarter extra clothing and other articles could be sent. However it would appear that the majority of these private 'next of kin' parcels were 'lost' in transit and those that did arrive took at least two months to reach their destination.

Inside a POW hut at Stalag IVB Muhlberg, 1943.

(drawn by Ray Newell and reproduced with his kind permission.)

As the war progressed, rail and road links in Germany were the targets of the allied bombers. Increasingly little non military equipment and freight was on the move. So, by the time Piper Willis arrived at Stalag IVB individual weekly food parcels were being allocated[34] at the rate of one between nine every fortnight. In short, the bare necessities were in very short supply and luxuries were non existent.

Fate takes a hand

By no stretch of the imagination could bagpipes be deemed essential. They were not going to magically appear in a Red Cross parcel and Piper George Willis, on entering Stalag IVB in the spring of 1944, was resigned to seeing the war out without playing the pipes or even a practice chanter. But fate was to take a hand. George Willis subsequently recalled[35]:

At the gate through which we entered, stood a middle-aged German Obergefreiter – the tallest and thinnest man I had ever seen – who shouted out in English, "Ho ho! They've captured St. Patrick! Come here," he said, pointing to me. He had noticed the piper's badge on my sleeve. "Do you play the pipes?" he asked. I nodded. "Follow me," he said. Not knowing what was coming, I walked behind Slim as I later learned that this officer had been nicknamed by the P.O.W. boys.

The prison camp consisted of very long large huts and we entered one of these. It contained many three-tier bunk beds. Stopping beside one of them, where a prisoner was lying down, Slim kicked the wooden side of the bed. "Where's your pipes?" he asked of this prisoner. This I later discovered was Pipe Major Neil of the Queen's Own Cameron Highlanders, who had piped his battalion out of Tobruk when it fell. The Pipe Major got up and handed me his pipes. "Sorry, Jock," I said. "Don't worry – it's O.K." he reassured me.

Slim led me away to a sunken road within the camp and signaled to me to play. I blew up the pipes and as I tuned them. I was surprised at their excellent condition. "Good," said Slim. "Can you play the 'Bearing of the Grin', 'the Ministerial Boy' or 'the Peeler's Gloat' "?

I later discovered that he had gained what English he had in 1914-18 war when he himself had been a P.O.W. incarcerated in Ireland, near the Curragh. It was here that he had discovered his love of Irish music.

Up I blew and played for him the many Irish tunes he requested. He listened intently and with increasing pleasure, bordering on delight! As he listened he tapped his feet in time to the music, and nodded his head, which caused his helmet to wobble something awful. The recital went on for twenty minutes or so, and then we returned to the hut to give the pipes back, with thanks, to Pipe Major Neil.

We were to share these pipes for the next fourteen months until 11.15 a.m. on the 3rd. May 1945 when the Russian Cossack Army liberated the Camp[36].

The P.O.W. Artist

Fifty years later, Pipe Cpl. Willis saw[37] a coloured drawing in his daily newspaper of the very same Pipe Major Neil, complete with the set of pipes they had shared in Stalag IVB. The artist was a Ray Newell, who had drawn a hundred or so such portraits whilst he too was a P.O.W. in Stalag IVB. He had managed to keep the drawings after he was liberated. On his return to civilian life he became a graphic artist of some repute.

He never made any mention of his prison camp work until asked, in the mid 1990s, to illustrate catalogues for the Tower of London. He produced his wartime work merely as evidence of his drawing skill. On seeing the drawings, the staff were so impressed that they organised an exhibition entitled 'Portraits from a Prison Camp'. Initially this was shown at the Royal Armoury Museum Leeds and then toured the country. A book[38] of the drawings was also published and Ray has subsequently given countless lectures on life as a P.O.W.

(RIGHT)
Pipe Major Neil of the Cameron Highlanders,
who, whilst a P.O.W,. shared his pipes with a P.O.W Piper
from the London Irish Rifles.

(drawn by Ray Newell and reproduced with his kind permission.)

(BELOW)
London Irish Pipers to the Fore!
The Pipes & Drums of 7th. Battalion R.U.R., September 1945,
with a front rank entirely of pipers who started the war as
members of the Pipes & Drums of the London Irish Rifles.

The First London Irish Rifleman Home from the War?

The War in Europe officially ended on 8th May 1945. However, by then the P.O.W. piper from the London Irish Rifles was already on his way home, having been liberated by the Russians on 3rd May. But moving across Europe against the invading Allied tide was not easy, and it was not until the 27th May that he got home to his wife Rose. On seeing him for the first time in nearly three years, she asked[39]

"Where have you been?"

Unbeknown to George his photograph had appeared in the press some days earlier, showing him being attended to by a W.V.S. volunteer. This was the first Rose knew her husband was free and more astonishingly that he was in the Country. She had been expecting him for the previous 48 hrs!

Despite the delay, Pipe Cpl. Willis was home months in advance of the rest of the Regiment. It was a source of great pleasure to George that when the Pipes & Drums of the 7th Bn. Royal Ulster Rifles beat retreat at Sheffield's Thanksgiving Week, he was a guest piper that day in a front rank that consisted entirely of pipers who had started the war in the London Irish Rifles' Pipe Band. So, in his own way, the London Irish P.O.W. Piper had his own L.I.R. victory parade – but thousands of miles away from his Regiment in Northern Italy.

Honours and the Toll

The Regiment's Second World War actions yielded a further 40 battle honours including Bou Arada, North Africa 1942-43, Sicily 1943, Sangro, Gariglliano Crossing, Anzio, Rimini Line, Argenta Gap and Italy 1943-45. These honours and other evidence suggests that the Regiment (either in the guise of the 1st. or 2nd. Battalion) was in the thick of the action for nearly three years. 747 London Irish Riflemen lost their lives. It has not been possible to establish the number of wounded or captured.

D-Day Dodgers

Before the war had even ended, the service and sacrifice by all the Allied troops who had remorselessly fought their way up the length of Italy, had already been dismissed by the widespread application of the nickname 'The D-Day Dodgers' - an implication of cowardice and avoidance of the 'real' war in France.

The expression originated[40] in correspondence between a Private in The Royal East Kent Regiment (the Buffs) and Lady Nancy Astor M.P. His letter was signed 'D-Day Dodgers' and she, assuming it was a humorous nickname like 'Desert Rats', began her reply "Dear D-Day Dodgers", only to find that it was soon being put around that during a Parliamentary debate[41] she had cast this odious slur on the troops in Italy. This was not surprising as many viewed her as an American born, sharp-tongued, wealthy noblewoman.

Those veterans who survived the Italian Campaign point out that two days before the first Allied soldier landed in Normandy, they were entering Rome. They had already been fighting in Italy for nine long months (and before that many, including the London Irish Rifles, had seen action North Africa and Sicily). These veterans would also remind the reader that the Italian Campaign cost[42] the Germans more casualties (556,000) than it did the Allies (312,000), and it tied down German divisions that would otherwise have fought elsewhere, some of them no doubt in Normandy.

But at the time, this information was not available and satire was the only weapon in the troops' armoury against the slur of dodging D-Day. Not for the first time[43], Lady Astor was to find herself featuring in a parody of a well known song. To the enormously popular melody of 'Lili Marlene', an Officer in the 51st Highland Division wrote[44] the following words:

> Dear Lady Astor, you think you know a lot
> standing on that platform and talkin' tommy rot
> you're England's sweetheart and her pride
> we think your mouth's too bloody wide
> that's from your D-Day Dodgers in sunny Italy.

The song rapidly became popular with the 8th Army and verses were added as it spread throughout the allied forces in Italy. Additional verses included:

> We are the D-Day Dodgers, way out in Italy,
> Always on the vino, always on the spree.
> We didn't land with Eisenhower
> So they think we're just a shower.
> For we're the D-Day dodgers out here in Italy.

Here's to Lady Astor, our pin up girl out here;
She's the dear old lady, who sends us such good beer
And when we get our Astor band
We'll be the proudest in the land,
For we're the D-Day dodgers out here in Italy.

We fought into Agira, a holiday with pay;
Jerry brought his bands out, to cheer us on our way,
Showed us the sights and gave us tea,
We all sang songs, the beer was free,
We are the D-Day Dodgers, in sunny Italy.

Cassino and Anzio were taken in our stride,
We didn't really fight there, we went there for the ride.
Sleeping till noon and playing games,
We live in Rome with lots of dames.
We are the D-Day Dodgers, in sunny Italy.

On our way to Florence, we had a lovely time,
We drove a bus from Rimini, right through the Gothic Line.
Then to Bologna we did go,
We all went swimming in the Po,
We are the D-Day Dodgers, in sunny Italy.

In verse after verse, the troops lampooned their supposed holiday in the Mediterranean, before reminding Lady Astor, in the last stanza, of all the Allied graves which contained their fellow 'D-Day Dodgers' who would stay in 'Sunny Italy' forever. The poignant final verse, which goes straight to the heart, was as follows:

Look around the mountains in the mud and rain,
You'll find the scattered crosses, some which bear no name.
Heartbreak and toil, and suffering gone,
The boys beneath and slumbering on.
They are the D-Day Dodgers, who stay in Italy.
They are the D-Day Dodgers, who stay in Italy.

References:

1. The main source for this chapter was *The London Irish at War* published by The Regimental Association, 1949 but no longer in print. A copy is however available for inspection on the Internet at http://rurmuseum.tripod.com/star
2. *History of the Royal Ulster Rifles* by Lt.-Colonel M. J. P. M. Corbally.
3. http://news.bbc.co.uk/1/hi/uk/765004.stm
4. http://www.adls.org.uk/
5. *The Emerald* No.58; page 8.
6. *The Emerald* No.58; page 8.
7. *The Emerald* No.29; page 35.
8. *The Emerald* No.57.
9. op. cit. *The London Irish at War*; page 31.
10. *The Emerald* No.34; page 34.
11. letter from Miss Richards dated 17 November 2003
12. http//nfo.net/brit/bh3.html
13. letter from George Donnelly dated 25 November 2003
14. op. cit. *The London Irish at War* at War page 39.
15. unpublished reminiscence of George Willis dated September 2003
16. op. cit. *The London Irish at War:* page 44.
17. op. cit. *The London Irish at War*: page 45 onwards.
18. op. cit. *The London Irish at War*. page 69 onwards.
19. op. cit. *The London Irish at War*; page 94.
21. www.spartacus.schoolnet.co.uk/FWWhallEG.htm
22. op. cit. *The London Irish at War* pages 78, 81, 91, 115 &176.
23. *Daily Telegraph* Obituary for Sir James Henry Bt. February 1997.
24. op. cit. *The London Irish at War*; page 193.
25. op. cit. *The London Irish at War*; page 169.
26. *The London Irish at War* page 171.
27. *The Drum* by Hugh Barty-King published for *The Royal Tournament* 1988 page 114.
28. op. cit. *The London Irish at War*; page 172.
29. op. cit. *The London Irish at War*; page 178.
30. quote from President H.S Truman (www.trumanlibrary.org/educ/germany)
31. *The Prisoner of War* Vol.3 No.27.
32. *The Prisoner of War* Vol.3 No.31.
33. Organisation of the British Red Cross and the Order of St. John of Jerusalem: letter ref PW/100A/42.
34. *The Emerald* No.49; page 15.
35. A fuller description of Piper Willis' time as a P.O.W. appeared in editions no 48 to 51 of *The Emerald*.
36. *The Emerald* No.50; page 26..
37. *The Emerald* No.55; Portraits from a Prison Camp.
38. *Portraits from a Prison Camp* by Ray Newell; published by the Royal Armouries Museum 1998.
39. *The Emerald* No.52; page 10.
40. *Nancy Astor: Portrait of a pioneer* by John Grigg; published by Sidgwick & Jacksom 1980; page 167.
41. There is no record in Hansard of Lady Astor ever making this statement in Parliament.
42. http://www.bbc.co.uk/history/war/wwtwo/d_day_dodgers_01.shtml
43. In 1926 she was greeted with a none to complementary song called 'Lovely Lady Astor' when she asked the miners of Esh Winning to take a pay cut (see http://www.wcml.org.uk/culture/songs_miners.htm); whilst in 1935 she featured in a song about Harry Pollitt, the then General Secretary of the Communist Party (see http://www.theoldie.co.uk/feature01_harrybolshie.html)
44. http://news.scotsman.com/topics.cfm?tid=1005&id=569292004

The Post War Years (1945-1968)

On 8th May 1945 at 15.00 hrs. Winston Churchill, the British Prime Minister, announced that war in Europe would end at midnight. However the cessation of hostilities was not the end of action for either the 1st. or 2nd. Battalions of the London Irish Rifles. From the outset both Battalions were heavily employed in what was euphemistically called 'peace keeping duties'.

Immediate Post War Security Duties

On 9th May, barely hours after the end of the war, the Irish Brigade (still including 2nd. Bn. L.I.R.) were moved into Carintha, an area of lower Austria with, at that time, somewhat flexible borders with Italy and Yugoslavia. The task was to 'enforce' the peace. However it was not a straightforward job. Firstly there were wave after wave of troops from the East (predominantly German and Croat soldiers) seeking to surrender to the British or Americans rather than to the Russians. In addition there were some 21,000 White Russian Cossacks who had retreated from the south after fighting for the German Army in Italy. Then there were Tito's Partisans racing towards the East to get back to their Country (and in the process colliding with the Quislings trying to escape from it). There were also Bulgarian and Hungarian detachments located in the area.

Brigadier Scott[1] was to say: "Nobody had the least idea what was going to happen next, or where it was going to come from .... These scallywags would cut each others throats. When you are in a complete mix up like this the British soldier reaches his peak. The tremendous prestige of the British Army can only be grasped when one sees its effect at first hand.....The one thing nobody was prepared to do was have a row with the British."

By the end of May the Balkan troubles started to subside. When July cam, the 2nd. Battalion was withdrawn to Ossiacher Lake, Austria. The autumn saw the 2nd. Bn. disbanded and its details absorbed into the 1st. Bn.

Meanwhile the 1st. Battalion had been in the disputed frontier region of Italy and Yugoslavia known as the Venezia Giulia. Here their task was a little easier as there were only two parties in dispute, namely Italy and Yugoslavia. There were numerous troublesome civilian demonstrations by both elements which, as reported[2] at the time, were only united in their enjoyment of the Pipes & Drums. The 'Venezia Giulia Crisis' was to keep the 1st. Battalion in the region for over a year.

In the summer of 1946, Field Marshal Alexander paid the London Irish a farewell visit. After Sandhurst his military career had started as a second lieutenant in the Irish Guards. By 1944 he was Commander in Chief of all Allied forces in Italy. It was reported[3] that his visit began with the Pipes and Drums of the London Irish Rifles greeting him with his old regimental march 'St. Patrick's Day' and when he left, he did so to the strains of 'Let Erin Remember'. He was later to be the Honorary Colonel of the London Irish Rifles.

The Band that Vanished

History records[4] that at the end of 1946 the London Irish Rifles were withdrawn to Rimini and disbanded. "Those remaining were immediately amalgamated with the London Scottish. When the Territorial Army was reconstituted. (1 January 1947) the London Irish Rifles were reformed at the Duke of York's and the Pipes and Drums were immediately resuscitated at an effective strength."

Research for this book has shown this is not the complete picture. During 1946 the number of men on the strength of the London Irish Rifles steadily declined as more and more men were demobilised and returned home. The Band's numbers were however maintained by recruiting from the ranks of those who remained, and there were plenty of volunteers. As one ex-rifleman of this era said[5], "it was better to drill with the pipes than a rifle".

It is true, as history records, that at the end of 1946, the London Irish Rifles were withdrawn to Rimini and disbanded. But as Piper Patrick Arlow recalls[6] those pipers and drummers still with substantial time to serve were transferred 'en masse' to 1st. Battalion Royal Ulster Rifles. However not a badge was changed, nor an item of uniform replaced. This Band looked like the London Irish Rifles and sounded like the London Irish but their demob papers showed they were officially Royal Ulster Rifles for the remainder of their army service.

For the next year or so, the 'Rimini Remnants' of the Pipes and Drums of the London Irish Rifles with Jackie Shanahan as Pipe Major (see page 106) were in Austria as the Royal Ulster Rifles. When garrison duty was undertaken in partitioned Vienna, the Regiment beat retreat every Sunday in the famous gardens of Schonbrunn Palace. These occasions featured both the L.I.R. Pipe Band and the R.U.R.'s Regimental Silver Band which had been transferred in from Jerusalem.

The Rimini Remnants
of the L.I.R. Pipe Band beat retreat in the formal gardens of the Schonbrunn Palace, Vienna, 1947.

Two hundred years earlier, a six year old Mozart had played here for Frederick the Great.

Links with the Royal Ulster Rifles

It was during the inter-war years that the ties between the London Irish Rifles and the Royal Ulster Rifles had become even closer and stronger. This association was officially recognised when the London Irish were first of all affiliated to, and then in 1929, became a part of the Corps of the R.U.R.

In 1937, following the abolition of the London Regiment (on yet another reorganisation of the Territorial Army), the full designation of the Regiment became 'The London Irish Rifles, the Royal Ulster Rifles'.

Prior to the Second World War, the R.U.R. itself did not have the pipes, although its affiliated T.A. Battalion (the London Irish Rifles) had had them since 1906. During the Second World War the piping expertise of the London Irish Rifles was used to establish several R.U.R. pipe bands including those for its 1st. Bn., 7th Bn. and 70th Young Soldiers Battalion.

The Second World War had shown the R.U.R. the value of a Pipe Band and when it was announced in 1948 that the three Regular Army Irish Regiments were to constitute the North Irish Brigade, the opportunity was seized by the R.U.R to officially form its own peacetime Pipe Band. This enabled them to fall in line with the other two regiments of the new Brigade (i.e. the Royal Irish Fusiliers and the Royal Inniskilling Fusiliers) both of whom had had pipe bands since the early part of the century.

The R.U.R. Regimental Pipe Band was formed[7] in 1948 from the nucleus of the Pipes and Drums of the L.I.R. 'Rimini Remnants'. The next year the new North Irish Brigade published its Book of Irish Pipe Music which was compiled with the help of the London Irish Rifles. This pipe music manual is still used to this day.

In 1954, the R.U.R received the freedom of the City of Belfast and a strong detachment of the L.I.R. went to Ireland for this ceremonial occasion. In crisp brilliant sunshine 20,000 people saw[8] the parade, which included the Massed Pipe Bands of the Queen's University Training Corps and the London Irish Rifles, with 'Kevin' the L.I.R. wolfhound mascot at their head.

Five years later, when the London Irish Rifles celebrated its centenary, the R.U.R., and its pipe band, took part in the celebrations and presented the Regiment with a superb pipe banner (see page 65).

In 1968 the Royal Ulster Rifles, the Royal Irish Fusiliers and the Royal Inniskilling Fusiliers were combined to form the Royal Irish Rangers.

In 1992 the Royal Irish Rangers joined with the Ulster Defence Regiment to form the Royal Irish Regiment. At the same time, with the formation of the London Regiment, the London Irish Rifles ceased to be a part of the Rangers.

Throughout all these amalgamations there has been a close bond between the L.I.R. Band and the successors to the Pipe Band of Royal Ulster Rifles. To this day there remains mutual support between the bands. The continued expertise of the L.I.R. musicians is in no small part due to the training provided by the R.U.R at its Ballymena Barracks and, in the past decade, by the visits to the London Irish of R.U.R. Pipe Major Brian Kidd.

Since 1969 the L.I.R Band has commemorated its bond and musical camaraderie with the R.U.R. Band by wearing silver buttons on its tunics instead of the traditional black L.I.R buttons. The motif on these silver buttons (see page 123) is that on the original R.U.R Pipe Band buttons.

The London Irish Rifles
receive the Freedom of the Borough
of Chelsea on the occasion of the
Regiment's Centenary in 1959.

Centenary of the Regiment

The year 1959 saw the Centenary of the London Irish Rifles. Such was the magnitude of the occasion, the BBC broadcast a twenty minute documentary on the Regiment and the London *Evening News* ran a series on the L.I.R. every day for a week. The Freedom of the Borough of Chelsea was also granted to the Regiment.

The highlight and focus of the celebrations was the Regimental Ball for All Ranks held at the Chelsea Town Hall. It commenced on the eve of the Centenary date itself but ran into the early hours of the morning of the 5th December. It was reported[9] that, "excitement mounted as midnight approached, and when at last the Pipes & Drums appeared, they led the assembled throng round and round the floor as the hour struck and the Regiment became 100 years old".

The Band was heavily involved in all the Centenary festivities and so it is fitting that by common consent,[10] "one of the most successful events of the year was the Regimental Luncheon". At this function the Royal Ulster Rifles presented the Regiment with a superb pipe banner, produced by the Royal College of Needlework. On one side was depicted the R.U.R badge and battle honours, on the other side the L.I.R badge and battle honours. As the Pipe Major of the wartime 2nd. Bn., it was fitting that Archie Evans was chosen for the honour of playing the pipes with the new banner.

Pipe Major Archie Evans
receives the Centenary Pipe Banner
from Brigadier Good of the Royal
Ulster Rifles.

Pipe Major Archie Evans

Archie Evans enlisted in the London Irish Rifles in 1933. Already a piper with the Great Western Railwayman's Pipe Band, he joined the L.I.R. Band straight away. He was a leading light of the 2nd. Bn., serving[11] throughout the Second World War as its Pipe Major and C.S.M. of its H.Q Company. He saw action in North Africa, Sicily, Italy and Austria. Under his leadership the 2nd. Bn. Pipe Band made many friends with the other Regiments of the Irish Brigade and amongst the Italian villagers in the mountains through which the Battalion fought.

Mercifully the War spared him and he continued to serve the Regiment. On the reformation of the Territorial Army Regiment in 1947, he helped Johnny Franklin to resuscitate the Pipes and Drums to an effective strength. Once this was achieved he held a succession of posts in the Regiment. As a result of his long service he held the Territorial Army Efficiency Medal with four bars, a rare distinction. In 1963 he was presented with the Territorial Army Meritorious Certificate by Field Marshal Earl Alexander of Tunis[12]. For over twenty five years he was also the General Secretary of the Regimental Association.

He was well known for his dry sense of humour and for being terse and to the point. However it was said that he would always give encouragement to anyone who tried to give of his best.

To Honour and Remember.
The Band leads the ranks of London Irish First World War survivors through the streets of Loos, fifty years on from the Battle.

Pilgrimage to Loos

The 50th Anniversary of the Battle of Loos was commemorated[13] in 1965 with a pilgrimage by 52 L.I.R. survivors. At the start of the First World War they had been light hearted youngsters but "now in the autumn of their lives they were attending their last parade; proudly and grimly they stood, men who had continually confronted and shared the risks and horrors of war but who had been spared."

The Pipe Band were honoured to be part of the accompanying party and featured throughout the weekend of remembrance. No performance was more moving than the blessing of the war memorial panel to the London Irish Rifles at Dud Corner Cemetery. At the conclusion of the service[14] "the Buglers sounded reveille, followed by a silence and then the pipers played the lament - its plaintive and haunting notes penetrating the soul. There was applause, which seemed longer than usual – then the last post rang out. It was a heart breaking moment."

References:

1. *The London Irish at War* published by The Regimental Association, 1949; page 216.
2. *The Story of the London Irish Rifles* edited Major R Cocburn M.B.E,
        published (1984) by the L.I.R. Regimental Association; page 42.
3. op. cit. *The London Irish at War*; page 218.
4. op. cit. R. Cocburn; page 40.
5. letter from Piper Patrick Arlow dated 16/2/04
6. op. cit. Piper Arlow
7. *The Irish Regiments 1683-1999* by R.G.Harris revised H.R.Wilson
        published Spellmount, 1999; page 156..
8. *The Emerald* No.10.
9. *The Emerald* No.16; page 9.
10. *The Emerald* No.16; page 8.
11. *The Emerald* No.44; Obituaries.
12. *The Emerald* No.20.
13. *The Emerald* No.22; Loos Commemorative Issue.
14. *The Emerald* No.22; Sydney Stadler page 10.

The Regimental Association Takes Control (1969)

In 1967 the Territorial Army was reorganised again and the London Irish Rifles was reduced to a Company of the Royal Irish Rangers: this latter title arising from the amalgamation of the Royal Inniskilling Fusiliers, the Royal Ulster Rifles and the Royal Irish Fusiliers.

Now, a mere Company, the L.I.R. was no longer entitled to a Regimental Band. This meant[1] the T.A. Company could not continue to be responsible for the Band. It was no longer possible for the Company Officers to find time from training duties to administer the Band. Also, as the Band was no longer part of the official establishment, there was no financial allowance available; nor was it possible to obtain further supplies of kit and instruments through army channels.

The General Management Committee of the Regimental Association carefully examined the problems involved, especially the financial outlay that might be required to ensure the Band's continued existence. Regulations were studied, there was correspondence with the Ministry of Defence and the advice of General Bredin was sought. It was finally agreed with the MoD that, although in the future the Band would be of a civilian nature, it would be allowed to function as a Military Band to support 'D' Company on all possible occasions. Furthermore the Band was permitted to wear its traditional uniforms on parade provided there was effective control exercised through a responsible and reliable Band President.

The responsibility for the Band was assumed by the Regimental Association in December 1969. Immediately after the momentous decision Major Rodney Cockburn was elected Band President. He at once formed an interim executive Committee in order to ensure that the take-over could be accomplished right away.

At this stage it was clear that there was no money in the Band Fund and no income-generating engagements had been arranged for the coming year. Uniforms were worn out and much of the kit and instruments needed repair. The Regimental Association launched a 'Save the Band Fund'. The response to the many pleas, written by the Association's Chairman Geoff Jenkins and produced by Charlie Self, a long standing Committee member and the Association's printer, produced a phenomenal response.

Less than a year later, the Band President was very upbeat and *The Emerald* reported[2] that:

> Far more progress had been made in the first six months of the Association's control than he ever thought possible. A very varied list of engagements had been carried out with great success: playing flat out marching down the Mall escorted by a tremendous crowd; entertaining 2,500 people at the Hammersmith Open Air Theatre; leading the entire Carnival parades at Slough and Waltham Cross.

He recalled the very important and very public parade by the Disbanded Irish Regiments Service at the Cenotaph. This parade was played down a Whitehall free of traffic, watched by mass crowds on the pavement: all members, particularly the buglers outstanding. Also true to its commitment, the Band had also supported 'D' Company since the Association had assumed responsibility for the Band.

He was proud to announce that the uniform was once again that of the London Irish Rifles; black buttons, St. Patrick's blue linings to the capes, the blue hackle and badge worn over the right eye, the caubeen pulled over the left ear All Uniforms had been checked and repaired by the official tailor (a new innovation), a further supply of capes, kilts and tunics had been obtained, mainly through the kindness and help of Major Johnny Bull of the Ministry of Defence. Pipers' badges, belts, socks, shoes, reeds and many other items had been purchased. The drums had been overhauled, the labour and technical know-how supplied by Andy Ridler.

He was pleased that the experienced body of musicians the Association had inherited from the Army had absorbed, in complete harmony, those recruited to increase the musical base of the Band from which the future could be planned.

Most of the musicians 'recruited to increase the musical base of the Band' were from civilian bands. Pipe Major O'Brien had realised that there were some advantages to no longer being an army band. In particular new musicians would not be required to be members of the Territorial Army - they would not have to meet the T.A.'s rigorous physical requirements. In future all that would be necessary was the musician could play his (or her) instrument whilst marching (hopefully) in step.

Overnight the potential pool of available musicians had been significantly increased. The long term survival of the Pipes & Drums of the London Irish Rifles appeared guaranteed as Pat O'Brien started recruiting pipers and drummers from other civilian bands. Notable amongst these were:

Chris Burt (Borough Pipe Band);
Archie MacMasters (Tower Hill Pipe Band);
Mick O'Malley (Tower Hill Pipe Band);
Jim Powell (Borough Pipe Band);
George Willis (Deptford Irish Pipe Band).

Between them these were to give over a hundred year's service to the Association's Band during the period 1970 to 2000.

It is worth noting that the 1968 Army reforms reduced the number of Regimental Bands in the British Army to 63. After the 1994 Army reforms there were just 29 officially established army bands left. Fortunately by this time the L.I.R. Regimental Association had already been funding and managing the Pipes & Drums of the London Irish Rifles for a quarter of a century. Thus, irrespective of government policy the future of this 'civilian band' was already guaranteed.

In the early years of the Association's stewardship of the Band it is clear that many, many people helped by way of donations, supporting fund-raising events or using their contacts to obtain discounted (or better still free) equipment or parts.

Andy Ridler, 1972.
A Scot, who joined the Gordon Highlanders as a boy drummer. After Second World War service, he played with the London Scottish but then transferred to the London Irish Rifles in 1951. He became devoted to the Regiment and played in the L.I.R. Band for 27 years.
It was Andy who totally overhauled the drums for the Association in 1970 and trained up the new intake of drummers.

Major Rodney Cockburn M.B.E.
who transformed a depleted and
insolvent outfit into the successful
Pipe Band that exists today.

Nobody wanted to see the Pipes & Drums of the London Irish Rifles disappear.

The leadership and hard work of the Band President Major Rodney Cockburn and Pipe-Major Pat O'Brien provided a focus and drove along all those seeking to retain the Band. These two laid the foundations for the modern era of the Pipes & Drums of the Regimental Association of the London Irish Rifles – an era which saw the Band go from strength to strength whilst other regimental bands were disappearing.

Major Rodney Cockburn M.B.E.

Rodney Cockburn enlisted into the Second Battalion of the London Irish Rifles when it was raised in 1939. After initial training he was commissioned within the Battalion. During the Second World War, he served in North Africa, Sicily, Italy and Austria. For most of this time he was H.Q. Company Commander and as such most of the Battalion's administration was in his hands.

It was said[3] of Rodney that he did his best to see that the men lacked for nothing – either in or out of the line. "No commander ever had to look over his shoulder in action for material needs .... after the holocaust of Cassino, the first message from Rodney was accompanied with a jorum [a large container] of rum."

In 1962 Major Cockburn was elected to the General Management Committee of the Regimental Association and two years later assumed responsibility from Geoff Jenkins for editing *The Emerald* (the journal of the Association). Rodney improved the style of the magazine and brought all the articles to life with his valuable experience of the national press. He was to edit *The Emerald* for 23 years and effectively wrote the publications for the Regiment's Centenary and then the 125th Anniversary (although he would say he merely edited them).

More famously, when the Association took responsibility for the Pipe Band in 1969, Rodney was unanimously elected the first 'civilian' Band President. His enthusiastic and innovative Presidency saw a rather depleted and insolvent outfit transformed into the flourishing and efficient Band that still exists today.

When nominated for the Band Presidency he was unsure whether to accept or not. As he told[4] those gathered at the Duke of York's for his retirement from the position 16 years later:

> I must have been a little slow in accepting because a voice in my ear said, "Go on! I will help you make it a success". The voice of course belonged to Pat O'Brien.

Pipe Major Pat O'Brien M.B.E.
Fifty years a London Irish Piper.

(RIGHT)
From Dog Major .....
**   .... to Pipe Major**
Pat O'Brien's earliest Band appearances, in 1940, were in charge of 'Tara', the Regimental Wolfhound.

(FAR RIGHT)
Rapidly becoming an excellent piper, he was appointed Pipe Major of 7th. Battalion R.U.R Band in 1943.

(BELOW)
Michael 'Joe' O'Brien
was, for a short time, a piper with his elder brother Pat, in the post war L.I.R. Pipe Band.

Pipe Major Pat O'Brien M.B.E.

Pat originally played the flute in the Limehouse Drum & Fife Band before learning the pipes with the London Irish when he was transferred from 'D' Company to the Pipe Band in August 1939. Whilst learning the pipes, he was one of 'Tara's' first 'Dog Majors'. He soon became an excellent piper, and after seeing action during the evacuation of Dunkirk (see page 37), he was posted to the 8th Battalion Royal Ulster Rifles to help form their pipe band. However, that Battalion became an 'ack-ack' unit, and Pat's love of the London Irish and its pipes made him request[5] a return to the L.I.R. – a request which was granted.

Pat was on the move again in 1942, when he was selected with Len Franklin (see page 76) to form a pipe band in the 70th Battalion (Young Soldiers) L.I.R. at Wembley (see page 42). When this Battalion was disbanded, Pat found himself in the R.U.R. as a Pipe Sergeant in their 70th Battalion. In 1943 he was promoted to Pipe Major of the 7th Bn. R.U.R.

In 1945 be was offered the appointment of Pipe Major with the Royal Irish Fusiliers, but he decided to stay where he was, as he was due to be demobbed the following year. In 1947 he was back with the London Irish Rifles in the re-formed T.A. Battalion. Pat was soon promoted to RQMS. and naturally he helped out with running the Band (which for a short time after the war also included his brother Michael 'Joe' O'Brien.)

When the Band became the Regimental Association's responsibility in 1969, Pat worked tirelessly to build the Band up to full strength and lay the foundations of its current world wide reputation. He was appointed Pipe Major in 1971. Pat relinquished this position in 1986 but continued to parade with the Band at almost all its engagements until 1990, when he felt that he was not well enough to continue.

He became Band Vice President in 1974 – a title he continued to hold up to the time of his death in 1998. During all the years be was Band Vice President he kept its accounts and was its chief administrator. He was awarded the M.B.E. in 1993 for services to piping.

The Regimental Association of the London Irish Rifles

The preservation of the Band since 1969 has not only aided recruitment to the London Irish Rifles, it has also made a great contribution to maintaining pride and interest in the Regimental Association.

The spirit that was so evident during the First World War continued in the Old Comrades Association, which was founded in 1918. The Second World War reinforced the Association, particularly through its efforts to help those at the front. After the Second World War the Association flourished and in 1955 changed its name from an Old Comrades Association to a Regimental Association. Such was the post Second World War strength of the Association, it felt confident enough to take control of the Regimental Pipes & Drums when the MoD was no longer willing to fund the Band.

Since its formation the Association's chief purpose[6] has been the welfare of the ex-members of the Regiment. Over the years, the Association's welfare officers have worked tirelessly in helping those in need. Today that purpose is still the prime one, yet during its 86 years existence the Association has not neglected its many other duties including supporting and co-operating with the Regiment and promoting its history and achievements.

Today the Regimental Association of the London Irish Rifles, and its Band in particular, provides a natural public focus for the London Irish Rifles – past, present and to come.

References:

1. This chapter extensively draws on *The Emerald* Nos.27 & 28.
2. *The Emerald* No.27; page 5.
3. *The Emerald* No.44.
4. *The Emerald* No.42; page 39.
5. *The Emerald* No.55.
6. *The Story of the London Irish Rifles* edited Major R Cockburn M.B.E, published (1984) by the L.I.R. Regimental Association; page 46.

Chairmen of The London Irish Rifles' Regimental Association.

(CLOCKWISE)

Col. 'Dick' Richards (1926 -1954)

Captain Hugh Hynds (1954 -1964)

Geoff Jenkins M.B.E. (1964 -1999)

Major Tony La Roche T.D. (1999 - 2004)

Major John Fallis T.D. (2004 - present)

Modern Times
(1970-2006)

This chapter is one of the longer in the book. This is not because so much information was at our disposal – although it was! Nor because the 36 years it covers is over a third of the lifetime of the Band. No, its length is dictated by the remarkable success of the Pipes & Drums of the London Irish Rifles' Regimental Association since 1970.

Before describing the more memorable parades and performances given by the modern day Band, the requirement by the Ministry of Defence (see page 67) that the Pipes & Drums should function as a Military Band on all possible occasions should be remembered. This is part of the agreement that permits the Band to wear the Uniform of the London Irish Rifles.

In its role as a military band, the Pipes & Drums have three engagements indelibly logged in its annual calendar of events, namely accompanying the current L.I.R. Territorials and former members of the Regiment in their parades for:

Loos Sunday (the Sunday nearest to 25th September);
Remembrance Sunday (the Sunday nearest to 11th November);
and
St. Patrick's Sunday (the Sunday nearest to 17th March).

Above all other parades these three are the Band's *raison d'etre*.

Memorable Parades and Performances

The pages that follow are an attempt to reflect the phenomenal success of the Band in modern times. Space and time have been constraints and inevitably the selection is subjective. Significant parades or performances omitted are:

- The Albert, Barbican and Guild Halls;
- Belgian National Horse Show (1974);
- Leiden (1993) and Eijesden (1994) both in Holland;
- Battle of Fontenoy Commemoration Parade (1995);
- National Memorial Arboretum (1999);
- Royal Variety Performance (2001);
- 9/11 Service at the USA Embassy London (17 September 2001);
- Longueval Pipers Memorial (2002 and 2003);
- Combined Irish Regiment Parades (yearly);
- Burma Star Association Parades (regularly);
- Commemorative Visits to Battlefields and Cemeteries in France, Belgium and Italy.

Parades or performances do not always go to plan and so we have included brief sections labelled "To the Rescue" as examples of initiative saving the day and the Band's reputation.

The Lord Mayor's Show

Having taken responsibility for the Pipes & Drums in December 1969 (see pages 67 to 69), the Regimental Association of the London Irish Rifles spent the next year recruiting and training additional pipers and drummers as well as equipping the Band with new uniforms. As a result 1971 saw a bigger and better Band undertake a heavy and extensive programme of parades and performances, including participation in the hundred strong massed bands for the T.A.V.R.'s 'London Pride' Military tattoo.

However, it was the Band's appearance at the annual Lord Mayor's Show in November 1971 that established that it was back in business. It was reported[1] that "the numbers on parade were high; 19 pipers and 12 drummers, who with the tall martial Bugle Major leading gave the City a real Saturday morning treat".

Literally millions of people, courtesy of colour television which had started to establish itself nation-wide in the UK, saw a superb London Irish Rifles' Pipe Band. A Band that sounded good and looked good!

In the years that followed this epoch making appearance, the Band has been invited back to the Lord Mayor's Show time and time again. However it was the first appearance that was pivotal in reminding the world that the London Irish still had Pipes & Drums.

Bigger, Better and Back in Business!
After a decade of decline, the revitalised Band, now the responsibility of the Regimental Association, plays at the Lord Mayor's Show, London, 1971.

Piper Major Franklin B.E.M. plays for H.R.H. the Queen Mother

On the evening of 8th June 1981, in the presence of Her Royal Highness the Queen Mother, who took the Salute, the massed military, bugle and pipe bands of the Irish Regiments carried out the ceremony of Beating Retreat on London's Horse Guards Parade.

Despite no longer being an official band of the British Army, the L.I.R. Regimental Association Band was very proud to have eight of its pipers invited to be members of a 100-strong body of army pipers. But its deepest honour was to have its former Pipe Major Johnny Franklin named as the lone piper in preference to all the full time military pipers on parade that day. The event was described[2] as:

.... an occasion when all the regimental bands blended together, with only three day's practice, to produce a memorable spectacle of colour, movement and Irish music. Every stand was filled to capacity by an audience utterly stirred by an exact exhibition of precision marching, the formation of intricate patterns and circles, whilst at the same time the well known Irish airs and melodies resounded across the vast parade ground.

After a bugle fanfare the massed military bands, accompanied by the large bugle band, marched on to 'It's a long way to Tipperary' for their opening set. At the far end of the arena a long line of scarlet tunic clad Irish Guardsmen marched on and formed a backcloth which gave Horse Guards Parade the appearance of a vast stage. The bugle band then gave a dazzling display in quick time and were followed by the massed pipes and drums who marched on from under the archway to the stirring air 'The South Down Militia'.

**Pipe Major Franklin
as 'The Lone Piper'**
for the Irish Regiments Beating Retreat for the Queen Mother on Horse Guards Parade, London, 1981.

The massed pipe bands then played traditional Irish airs. The finale began with 'The Londonderry Air' and in the silence that followed that mournful tune the Lone Piper marched on. He was announced over the loudspeaker system as:

'Pipe Major John Franklin of the London Irish Rifles
who piped his regiment ashore at Anzio in 1943'.

He mounted the three step high dais in front of the royal box and then, facing the Queen Mother, piped 'Oft' in the Stilly Night'.

The ceremony drew to a close with Sunset and Retreat followed by the National Anthem. The Parade then marched off, to the strains of the various regimental marches. The last unforgettable memory of a magnificent display was the entire parade about to leave at the far end of Horse Guards playing 'Garryowen' the regimental march of the London Irish Rifles.

After the ceremony H.R.H. the Queen Mother shook hands and had a long talk with P/M Franklin. The Queen Mother told him that 'Oft' in the Stilly Night' was one of her favourite tunes. She congratulated him on his piping and wished him well for the future. She then asked if the set of pipes he had been playing were the same as he had used at Anzio to pipe the regiment ashore. The answer was, "yes, with some replacements".

By the time Johnny Franklin had been honoured as 'the Lone Piper' he was the best known Pipe Major in London. He joined the Territorial Army Regiment of the London Irish Rifles as a 19 year old in 1928. By 1937 he had been appointed the Band's Pipe Major and as such featured in the December edition of the Territorial Magazine wearing full dress.

Throughout the Second World War Johnny was the Pipe Major of the 1st. Battalion's Pipe Band. On the reformation of the London Irish Rifles as a Territorial Army Regiment in 1947, he helped reinstate the Band, acting as its Pipe Major for a short period. The succession of Pipe Majors that followed him benefited from the fact that Johnny still played with the Band and his expertise was readily available. He was awarded the BEM in 1951 for his services to piping and played with the Band until the mid 1980's.

Johnny's brother Len Franklin was also a piper with the London Irish Rifles from 1937 until 1942. His war service started with the 1st. Battalions Band before being transferred to help establish the Pipe Band for the L.I.R. Young Soldiers Battalion (see page 42).

To the Rescue No. 1

At the 1979 Bromley Show, the Band's coach found its access to the assembly area barred by a locked barrier. It was³ "immovable; there was no way round. Time was running out!"

But all was not lost. In response to a request for help from the Pipe Major, a Band member came forward and calling on skills learned at the 'University of Life' picked the lock.

The way was cleared!

Faugh a Ballah!

(ABOVE)
Len Franklin.
P/M Johnny Franklin's younger brother was also a piper with the London Irish Rifles from 1937 to 1943.

(OPPOSITE)
The Queen Mother asks Pipe Major Johnny Franklin
if the set of pipes he is playing are the same as he used to pipe the Regiment ashore at Anzio in 1944.

Loos 70 years on

The 1980s saw many momentous military anniversaries: most notably the Tercentenary of the Royal Inniskilling Fusiliers (1989), the London Irish Rifles' own 125th Anniversary (1984), and the 50th Anniversary of the outbreak of the Second World War. However the consensus is that the outstanding event of the decade was the 70th Anniversary of the Battle of Loos (1985).

As the pinnacle of a weekend of commemoration, the town of Loos-en-Gohelle staged a *son-et-lumiere* spectacular in an open air amphitheatre which had been created in the slag heap area near the town. *Le Sablier et les Epis*, as the event was titled, was described[4] as:

> .... a most moving spectacle, depicting the history of the War from 1914 to 1918. Although the commentary was entirely in French, the L.I.R. visitors were able to understand the pageant which had been prepared and rehearsed by the people of Loos. It was of a highly professional standard and emphasised the futility of war.
>
> At the Finale, as the L.I.R. Band played, 93 year old Percy Tomlin was led out into the vast arena, where he found himself alone in the full brilliance of the spotlights – the sole representative, for those few moments, of the generation who fought in the First World War. Tremendous applause broke out and we were very moved to see Percy draw himself up proudly to attention to receive the ovation.

It was thought that with the passing of Percy in 1992, the Regiment lost its last living link with the First World War. However in 1998 the President of France announced that all living British First World War veterans who had fought in France, would be awarded the Legion d'Honneur. The Royal British Legion traced these men and in Croydon found London Irish Rifleman George Gadsby aged 100. Two days before his 101st birthday George received his award.

A veteran of the Somme, Ypres and Cambrai, George had kept a war diary which is now in the L.I.R. Regimental Museum. His entry for St. Patrick's Day 1918 is at page 150 of this book.

(LEFT)
Percy Tomlin, aged 93, takes centre stage at the 70th Anniversary of the Battle of Loos in 1985.

(RIGHT)
George Gadsby, aged 101 and the last London Irish survivor of the First World War, was presented with the French Legion d'Honneur by Col. Michel Perrodon, 1999.

(BELOW)
The Tomlin Family 1915. L.I.R. Sgt. Alfred Tomlin with sons L.I.Rfn. Percy, Royal Fusilier Herbert and Boy Scout Harold.

The Band Returns to the Vatican after 40 years

As part of the Regimental Association's 1987 visit to Italy it had been arranged that they should visit the Vatican and with luck have an Audience with the Pope, just as the Regiment had during the Second World War (see pages 52 and 53). They were not anticipating the select Audience afforded Heads of State but were expecting to be among the many thousands who throng the monthly Papal Audience. A member of the visit to the Vatican reported[5]:

> We possessed a very efficient 'Mr. Fixit' in the Band's Q.M. Dennis Mulqueen (see page 118), who had been to Rome a couple of days prior to the visit. He claimed to have everything in hand but we didn't know what to expect. Nonetheless we applied extra spit and polish to our uniforms just in case.
>
> When we arrived in St. Peter's Square, there were many other groups of musicians amongst the thousands awaiting admittance but we were ushered into the first of two courtyards where the Swiss Guards searched us and we were waved through to the second. Here we were searched again but on neither occasion thoroughly enough to discover what we had on under our kilts!
>
> Then the Vatican streamlined organisation took over and directed us into an enormous auditorium the size of the Albert Hall. As we marched nearly a hundred yard to our places in the very front row, we played a melody of Irish marches that reflected the long standing ecumenical nature of our Band.
>
> Immediately the Audience Chamber was full, a procession of Church dignitaries resplendent in their scarlet and black entered and then suddenly the Pope was there right in front of us. The warmth of his smile and strength of character made a great impression on me, and I am sure, on all of us.

The Vatican, 1987.
Pope John Paul II with Band President Major John Fallis and the Pipe Band of the Regimental Association of the London Irish Rifles.

Exchanging Second World War Stories?
Piper George Willis, this book's co-author, talks in broken Italian to Pope John Paul II. Drummer Barry King looks on.

After a short service in Latin, the various groups known to be in the audience were welcomed in their own language by the Papal Secretary. The London Irish, however, received a personal salutation by the Pope. He said, in English:

"A very special welcome to the Pipes & Drums of the
London Irish Rifles Regimental Association."

He also commended those, who like ourselves, had fought for humanity in the Second World War.

He then descended the steps and bestowed upon us his Papal Blessing. We responded by playing a hymn as an impressive finale to the Papal Audience.

But the Audience was not over as far as we were concerned. His Holiness wished to speak with us and came towards us. He spoke first to Major John Fallis, our Band President, and then with all of us individually, shaking the hand of every Band member. He told us we were 'Bella musica' and 'Magnifico'.

After presenting us all with rosary beads, he moved off to other groups. During his progress we played 'Oft in the Stilly Night', 'Amazing Grace' and 'The Skye Boat Song'. The acoustics of the audience chamber were ideally suited to pipes and drums. We played and sounded as if inspired.

The following day there were pictures in the Italian newspapers of the Pope talking to us. Unfortunately one described us as 'Musicians of the Irish Guards', but everything had gone so smoothly and successfully that we could overlook this small mistake. We felt a great deal of gratitude to Dennis Mulqueen for his efforts in bringing about so memorable an occasion.

The Inaugural Colours Ceremony for the new London Regiment.
The Duke of York's Barracks, 1997.

The New London Regiment

The new London Regiment, of which 'D' (London Irish Rifles) Company now forms a part, was ceremoniously inaugurated on 1st August 1993 with a full Regimental Parade at the Duke of York's Barracks, Chelsea. All the component units and their Regimental Associations took part and the military music was provided by the Massed Bands comprising the traditions being amalgamated in the new Regiment, namely:

> The Pipes & Drums of the London Scottish
> The Drum Corps of the City of London Fusiliers
> The Drum Corps of the Queens Fusiliers
> The Pipes & Drums of the London Irish Rifles
> (The Royal Green Jackets were not to join the Regiment until 1999.)

At the time the ceremony was described[6] as "a fabulous occasion", but four years later the spectacle was surpassed when the Regiment was presented with its inaugural Colours by H.R.H. the Duke of York.

The programme notes for 'The Colours' Ceremony reminded those attending that from the earliest recorded battles, armies had carried flags which symbolised their loyalty and served as rallying points in battle. By the early 17th century formal regimental flags had come into being and in 1751 a Royal Warrant decreed that only two Colours were to be carried by each regiment. These were the King's Colour bearing the 'Great Union Flag' and a Regimental Colour. These 'Colours' rapidly came to represent the spirit of a regiment, and served as a focus of pride to such an extent, that by 1882 they were considered too important to take into battle.

The consecration and presentation of the inaugural Colours to the new London Regiment on the 25th July 1997 was a spectacle of music and colour so vivid that those who were there that day, still recall the experience as if it were yesterday.

81

Bugle Major Brendan MacDonagh of the London Irish Rifles who, as the senior drum major on parade, led the Massed Pipes & Drums of the Commonwealth at the 1999 Royal Tournament.

The Royal Tournament

For many years the Royal Tournament was the world's largest military tattoo. Its origin[7] was an 'Assault-at-Arms' display at the Albert Hall in 1878. This was so successful, that the next year it was combined with the annual rifle display given by the Volunteer Forces (including the London Irish Rifle Volunteer Corps) on Wimbledon Common.

The following 25 years saw the event, now called the 'Grand Military Tournament and Assault at Arms', housed in the 10,000 seat Agricultural Hall. In 1884 Queen Victoria gave permission for the Royal prefix to be added to the title. Such was the attendance[8], as it became more spectacular and more popular, that it moved to Olympia in 1906, and the event was extended from fifteen to seventeen days. After moving to Earl's Court in 1950, the Royal Tournament drew audiences of 350,000 every year.

By the 1970s, however, cuts in production values to balance the books, meant the show was less and less spectacular and its popularity waned. In 1992 the show was cut from three weeks to two and 1999 saw the last ever Royal Tournament.

After participating in the embryonic Tournament on Wimbledon Common, the London Irish were not to appear again for over 120 years.

In 1996 the Band participated with others to form 'The Massed Pipes and Drums of the Irish Regiments'. At the time it was said[9] that it "was a first class performance and several letters of commendation were received including one from H.M. the Queen".

The Pipes & Drums of the London Irish Rifles must have impressed many people that year, because in 1999 the Royal Irish Regiment asked the London Irish to play with them again at the Royal Tournament – this time in 'The Massed Pipes and Drums of the Commonwealth'. However, before rehearsals started the Royal Irish Regiment were deployed to the Balkan Emergency and the United Kingdom contingent of the massed Bands was reduced to the London Irish Rifles, the Royal Irish Hussars and the Royal Artillery.

The Massed Pipes and Drums of the Irish Regiments comprised of 120 pipers and drummers, with five Drum Majors. Despite two of the Drum Majors being from the Regular Army, Bugle Major Brendan MacDonagh of the London Irish Rifles was selected to be the senior Drum Major on parade. At one performance, HRH the Prince of Wales lent over the barrier and said[10] to Brendan that he was "glad the London Irish had survived!" This was an obvious reference to the Strategic Defence Review that had seen the disappearance of the names of so many famous regiments.

The 1999 performances at Earl's Court constituted the final Annual Royal Tournament. It was poetic that, as one of the original participants in the embryonic tournament on Wimbledon Common in 1879, the London Irish Rifles were also to participate at that last Royal Tournament.

After a Finale at the Royal Tournament

The summer of 1999 was very hot and within the concrete confines of Earl's Court it was sweltering on parade and even hotter behind the scenes. Regular liquid intake by the performers was important to maintain hydration levels. London Irish Piper Maurice Links recalls taking liquid on board after one performance. He and Piper Louisa Rostant were:

> ... enjoying a glass or three in the company of one of the pipers from an Irish regiment of the regular army. In the presence of what he took to be part time amateurs this piper was extolling his own abilities, telling anyone who was in earshot how his fingers were those of a champion piper and were insured for thousands of pounds.

This cut little ice with the two L.I.R. pipers who had heard it all before. However, continuing to replace the liquid they had lost through piping in the sweltering, sixteen thousand seat arena, they raised their eyebrows, smiled knowingly and nodded sagely. Taking these gestures as signs of wonderment, the 'champion piper' settled down with his captive audience and unwittingly matched their consumption glass for glass, whilst he regaled them with his experiences.

Next day, when the Massed Bands assembled for the afternoon matinee performance, the 'champion piper' was nowhere to be seen. Enquires of his regimental colleagues revealed that whilst his highly insured fingers were intact, they were shaking so uncontrollably that he could not play the pipes. Needless to say the London Irish duo was having no such problems and performed to their usual high standard.

Nova Scotia (1998)

In 1998 the Pipes & Drums of the Regimental Association of the London Irish Rifles were invited[11] to represent the United Kingdom at the Nova Scotia International Tattoo. This is one of the World's largest events of its kind and draws an audience of over 60,000 every July in its 10-day run in Halifax, Canada. It has been described[12] as "a breathtaking musical spectacle of pomp, pageantry, energy and spirit, featuring over 2,000 military and civilian performers from all over the world".

The L.I.R. Band arrived in Canada note perfect, thanks to weeks spent practising the musical scores provided in advance. However the first week of the Band's three week stay was given to rehearsing with the other members of the 110 strong massed pipe bands (see photograph at page 134). It was during these intensive rehearsals that the extreme professionalism of the London Irish buglers caught the eye of the organisers and they were assigned the honour of signalling the start of the Tattoo for every performance.

Before the Tattoo's traditional Canada Day opening performance, the participants take part in Halifax's national day parade. On this occasion the London Irish Rifles formed a composite band with the members of the Fraser Holmes Memorial Ladies Pipe Band from Westville, Nova Scotia.

Apart for its performances at the Tattoo, the L.I.R. Band also gave many lunchtime open air performances around Halifax. At these the Band was able to give full vent to its traditional London Irish repertoire and invariably drew large crowds, in which ex-pats (of both British ana Irish origins) were easily identifiable by their moist eyes.

There was only one rostered day off during the time in Canada and the Band chose to relax by taking part in a pipe band competition. Of a field of seven, they were second to their friends of the Fraser Holmes Pipe Band.

The end came all too soon and the farewell parties continued until it was time to depart for the UK. The Band left Canada not only having made many friends, but also having enhanced the world wide reputation of the London Irish Rifles.

Nova Scotia Tattoo, 1998.
Bugle Major MacDonagh
with his counterpart Mike McGinley
from The Royal Canadian Mounted
Police.

To the Rescue No. 2

Remembrance Sunday 1979 saw the Band in trouble[13]. The Bass Drummer had been struck down with flu and his Deputy had just retired. As the Band assembled, the Pipe Major had pencilled in the Bugle Major or his Deputy to play the Bass Drum – but both reported sick that Sunday.

At short notice Piper Hughie Dymond offered to beat time.

The only time a London Irish drummer has paraded wearing a kilt.

Ceremonial Duties at Buckingham Palace.

(ABOVE)
The Massed Pipes & Drums of the London Irish and the London Scottish lead out the 'Old Guard' from the Palace, 1996.

(BELOW)
Drummer Ted Weldin at the Palace, 1999.

Changing the Guard at Buckingham Palace

It is part of the folklore of the London Irish Rifles, that the Regiment provided the guard for the Royal Household at some stage before the Second World War. However extensive research has failed to substantiate this. In fact prior to 1996, the only contact the Band had with Buckingham Palace itself (as opposed to the Monarchy) was in 1982 when the Royal mews asked[14] for the loan of a bass drum to train young horses for ceremonial occasions – especially the Royal wedding due later that year. When the Palace was finished with the drum it was returned by special messenger – a royal coach drawn by two horses complete with driver and attendant.

However this was to change in 1996 when the London Regiment were ordered to guard Buckingham Palace and the Pipes & Drums of the Regimental Association were invited to augment the London Regiment's Band for this prestigious duty.

So on a sunny July day, the London Regiment (including 'D' Company the London Irish Rifles), accompanied by its Massed Pipes & Drums, marched from Wellington Barracks to form the 'New Guard' for the Palace. In a ceremony[15] dating back to 1660, the guards were changed in the Palace forecourt to the accompaniment of Celtic marches and airs. After leaving a detachment at Buckingham Palace, the 'New Guard' and its Band, marched to St. James's Palace where it would be based for the next 48 hours.

So successfully did the Regiment fulfil its security and ceremonial duties in 1996, it was ordered three years later to guard the Palace again. Once again the Pipes & Drums of the London Irish Rifles were honoured to be invited to participate in this world renowned ceremony.

Making History at the Tower of London, 2000. The first civilians to take part in the centuries' old Ceremony of the Keys. London Irish Buglers (LEFT TO RIGHT): Tom Raper, Roy Clarke, Tom Metcalf & Don Henchey.

Making History at the Tower of London

In recent years the London Irish Rifles have paraded so many times, and the Association's Pipe Band played so often at the Tower of London, that it has become a second home. So much so, that permission was granted for the Regiment to hold its 2003 St. Patrick' Day Parade at the Tower - an honour that was repeated in 2005 (see photograph on page 150).

However, the most memorable appearance at the Tower by the Band had a very small audience. This was because it was participating in the Ceremony of the Keys. This is the traditional locking up of the Tower of London. It is one of the oldest and most colourful ceremonies of its kind, having taken place in much the same form for over 700 years.

Since the restoration of the Monarchy in 1660, every night[16] without fail, the Chief Warder emerges, at exactly seven minutes to 10 o'clock, from the Byward Tower. He is wearing his long red coat and Tudor bonnet, carrying in one hand a candle lantern and in the other hand the Queen's Keys.

He proceeds round the Tower and locks in sequence first the Traitors' Gate and then the great oak gates of the Middle and Byward Towers.

At the Bloody Tower a sentry challenges, "Who goes there?" The Chief Warder answers: "The Keys." "Whose Keys?" the sentry demands. "Queen Elizabeth's Keys." "Pass Queen Elizabeth's Keys. All's well" is the sentry's final rejoinder.

The party then proceeds through the Bloody Tower archway and up towards the steps where the main guard is drawn up. The Chief Warder and escort halt at the foot of the steps and the officer in charge gives the command to present arms. The Chief Warder moves two paces forward, raises his Tudor bonnet high in the air and calls, "God preserve Queen Elizabeth." The guard answers "Amen." Queen's House and the guard is dismissed, the 'Last Post' is sounded. When the Buglers of the London Irish Rifles' Band performed this task in 2000, they were told afterward that they were the first Territorial Regiment to be afforded this historic honour. None of the Band had the heart to confess that they were not even Territorials but civilian members of a Regimental Association Band.

Unlike the nightly Ceremony of the Keys, the Installation of the Constable of the Tower takes place just once every five years. It too can only be viewed by a small number of officially invited guests of the Yeoman Body and other participants.

It has been said[17] that, with its array of colourful uniforms and rousing marches, this event stands tall on pomp and circumstance. It is certainly something to behold and in October 2001 the London Irish Rifles were privileged to take part in this ancient ceremony which dates back to 1078. The Regiment's Honorary Colonel, General Sir Roger Wheeler was being installed as the 158th Constable, so the main guard and Band was formed by the London Irish Rifles and the Royal Irish Regiment (whose predecessor regiment, the R.U.R., Sir Roger had once commanded).

To the Rescue No. 3

The annual Leiden Festival in Holland celebrates the defeat of the Spanish in the 16th century. For the 1993 parade, the Pipes & Drums of the London Irish Rifles had been given the honour of leading the procession, which that year included three bands from the British Regular Army as well as bands from all over Europe.[18]

But as the procession was about to move off, Jim Powell, the Bugle Major, became ill and was rushed to hospital. Fortunately another Jim [Major MacLeod - the Band President] was accompanying the Band in his No, 1 uniform and had to fall in and take the stick!

Farewell to the Duke of York's: Welcome to Connaught House

In January 2000 the London Irish Rifles marched out of its Duke of York's Headquarters in the King's Road, Chelsea for the last time.

In 1859 the initial meeting to discuss the formation of a London Irish Volunteer Corps had been held in Essex Street (off the Strand). Bigger meetings to firm up the idea were subsequently held in Morley's Hotel, Trafalgar Square. Once the Corps had been authorised, the first drills were held in Hungerford Hall (which was later to become part of Charing Cross Railway Station) and a H.Q. established at 7 John Street, off the Strand. Monthly musters were initially held at Burlington House and then at Somerset House.

Over the next fifty years the Regiment remained based in the vicinity of The Strand until 1911 when it was moved to what had recently become known as the Duke of York's Barracks. Previously, since 1802, these buildings had housed the Duke of York's Military School – a boarding school for the sons of soldiers, especially those soldiers who had been killed or seriously wounded on active service.

From 1911 to 2000 the Duke of York's was home to the London Irish Rifles. It is often said that 'home is where the heart is' and this was particularly true for London Irish Riflemen. They had left for action from the 'Duke's'; they had returned to it victorious; and the building had housed the memorial to their fallen comrades. The building evoked a wealth of memories for the extended community that consists of the soldiers, family and friends of the London Irish Rifles. They had celebrated and remembered there. But this was for nothing when the 1998 Strategic Defence Review decided to disperse the Territorial Army Units housed

From Chelsea.....
.....to Camberwell.
After 90 years at the Duke of York's Barracks, the London Irish Rifles leave their Chelsea H.Q. for the purpose-built premises in Camberwell named after the Duke of Connaught, who for over 70 years was the London Irish Rifles' longest serving Honorary Colonel.

at the Duke of York's and sell off the buildings. On 22 January 2000, in the words[19] of the editor of *The Emerald*:

> We marched out of the Duke of York's with the Pipes and Drums leading 'D' Company with bayonets fixed, followed by the Cadets and the Regimental Association. Turning right out of the Duke's we marched, with police assistance, round Sloane Square, back along the King's Road and passing the Duke's where we gave an 'eyes left' to our President, Major General Purdon, at the gate.
>
> The parade was watched by many bemused shoppers and tourists. We then bore left down Smith Street and into the grounds of the Royal Hospital where we embussed into coaches for the journey to Camberwell Green.
>
> Here in a very different setting, we formed up again and set off for Flodden Road, where our Honorary Colonel, General Sir Robert Corbett, was waiting along with the Mayor of Lambeth to whom we gave an 'eyes right'. The Mayor then inspected the parade, speaking to nearly everyone and welcoming us all to the Borough of Lambeth. Then we all moved into our new headquarters and drill hall, the aptly named Connaught House.

This name Connaught House was appropriate because H.R.H. Prince Arthur, the Duke of Connaught (see page 28) had been the Regiment's Honorary Colonel for over seventy years from 1871 until his death in 1942. He had always kept in touch with the Regiment over the years, often leading it at its annual review.

The march down Camberwell New Road to Connaught House is shown in the colour plate at page 134 and has been commemorated by Pipe Sgt. Jim McCombie's stirring composition 'London Irish Rifles' Welcome to Connaught House'.

The Band at Connaught House.
(CLOCKWISE)

Friday night band practice;
The sign for Mulqueen's Bar – the Band's 'spiritual' home;
Practice over, this is for real.

Life President **Laurie Mansfield**   Hon. Chairman **Peter Prichard OBE**   Hon. Treasurer **Ray Donn**   Executive Administrator **Peter Elliott**

tender their congratulations to

The Pipes & Drums of the London Irish Rifles

on being selected to appear before

Her Majesty The Queen

on the occasion of

THE ROYAL VARIETY PERFORMANCE

Monday 26th November 2001
at the
Dominion Theatre

in aid of
The Entertainment Artistes' Benevolent Fund

eabf

The Silver Shamrocks Mini Band never appeared at the Royal Variety Performance. However it did enliven many L.I.R. social functions during the 1970s. The L.I.R. Pipe Band personnel who featured in the mini-band are detailed on page 99.

References:

1. *The Emerald* No.29; page 30.
2. *The Emerald* No.38; page 3.
3. *The Emerald* No.37; page 32.
4. *The Emerald* No.43.
5. *The Emerald* No.45.
6. *The Emerald* No.51; page 17.
7. http://ejmas.com/jmanly/articles/2001/jmanlyart_wolf2_0801.htm
8. www.worldofevents.net/em/em_history_19th.html
9. *The Emerald* No.53.
10. *The Emerald* No.56.
11. *The Emerald* No.55.
12. http://www.ihffilm.com/ihf/687.html
13. *The Emerald* No.37; page 20.
14. *The Emerald* No 39; page 35.
15. http://www.tourist-information-uk.com/buckingham-palace.htm
16. www.toweroflondontour.com/keys.html
17. http://www.camelotintl.com/tower_site/warders/157.html
18. *The Emerald* No.51; page 18.
19. *The Emerald* No. 57.

Drums and Bugles

The 1st. Battalion's Drums, Kent, 1940.

The tenor drummer in the centre of the photograph is Bill Jackson, who aged 90 in 2004 is the oldest known surviving Band member.

Note:
- the leather apron worn by the bass drummer;
- rope tensioned drums;
- only the bass and tenor drums are emblazoned.

Although the subject of this book is The Pipes & Drums of the London Irish Rifles, the word 'Drums' is often quickly passed over. Even worse, the Band's full title makes no recognition at all of the existence of Bugles in the Band.

This chapter explains the history and conventions behind the full title and seeks to redress the imbalance between drummers and pipers and pay due attention to the role of buglers in a rifle regiment's band.

The Evolution of Military Drums

The essence of a drum has not changed much since biblical times. Fundamentally it comprises of a vessel forming a resonant cavity, over which a thin membrane is tightly stretched and secured. This membrane is set in vibration by directly hitting it.

Drum innovations over the centuries have been few and far between. The most significant from a military perspective are:

- The use of drumsticks[1] rather than hands by the ancient Egyptians.
- The emergence[2], in Eastern Europe around the fourth century A.D., of the tabor – a small, double-headed drum. The drum hung on a loop over the forearm of the musician, who beat the rhythm with one hand while playing a melody on a pipe with the other. The Crusaders brought this drum to Western Europe in the eleventh century. Over the next three hundred years the tabor got bigger and bigger to meet military requirements.
- The development of the military field drum by the Swiss[3] in the 15th century. With its wooden shell drum, it was too large and too heavy to be hung over the forearm and was attached to a strap over the drummer's shoulder or tied to a belt round his waist.
- The use, from the 15th century onwards, of top and bottom hoops to apply tension to the skins. These hoops[4] were joined and tensioned by rope threaded in a 'Y' pattern and further tightened by pushing leather lugs up the 'Y'. 'Rod tension' drums using metal lug bolts to tighten the hoops were first[5] seen 1806.
- The introduction[6], in the 16th century, of multiple catgut strings (called snares) stretched across the bottom skin of the field drum. This changed the tone of a drum beat giving it a higher, crisper sound better suited to signalling on the battlefield.
- The adoption of 'Turkish Music' (see page 10) as time beaters by 17th century European military bands, gave rise to the use of the bass or 'Turkish' drum. Such drums were known to have existed from at least the 14th century and a 1502 painting by Carpaccio[7] shows a Turkish drummer with an instrument of similar proportions to the modern military bass drum. In this painting, the drum hangs at the drummer's breast where it is beaten with two thick wooden sticks. At a later stage one of the wooden sticks was replaced by a 'ruthe' (a small broom like implement made of twigs) which supplemented the main beat of the wooden stick. Still later felt beaters were introduced which produced a deep tone.
- The invention of the tenor drum (i.e. pitched between the bass and the side drums) and first used by the Royal Artillery[8] Band in 1834. A drum without snares, it has been described[9] as "a little marching kettledrum ...... beaten with soft headed drumsticks; it has a distinctive subdued tone of its own".

Drums and Fifes in the British Army

Drums had been part of the British Army since[10] at least the battle of Halidon Hill in 1333 and were used to signal tactical direction to companies on the battle field. Nearly 200 years later, it was Henry VIII who introduced the fife to the English army after hearing[11] fifes and drums of the Swiss mercenary Landsknechts directing the battle at the Battle of the Spurs in 1513. From henceforth a drummer/fifer appeared on the roll for each English company of 100 men used in subsequent campaigns of King Henry's reign.

Rope tensioned drum, 1916.

(BELOW)
The Regimental Crest
barely distinguishable on the above drum is a crowned Maltese Cross bearing a 'Tara' harp,

(BELOW)
A 'Drum Head' Service
using the drums of the London Irish as an altar. In the past Drum Heads also served as the site of courts martial in the field.

(TOP TO BOTTOM)

Rope tensioned side drum (1955.)

Rod tensioned side drum (1975.)

Emblazoned bass drum (1990.)

Successive monarchs kept the practice, although at some stage an extra musician was allocated[12] to 'flank' companies.

In contrast to some European armies, the British have no known record of the fife's use in battlefield service. It appears to be predominately used as an off battlefield timekeeper to regulate the soldier's day in camp or quarters. It signalled the start and end of the day, meal times etc – there being few clocks or time pieces commonly available until the 19th century.

The fife became a popular addition to the Army's everyday life. It helped break the monotony of the day, whether awaiting battle or moving by foot from A to B. In time the fife and drum became an essential 'mode of transport' to the line of march[13]. It was also a source of entertainment; leading soldiers' songs around campfires or in the guardroom.

The modern (as opposed to ancient) drumming era began in 1810 when a Samuel Potter, the Regimental Drum Major of the Coldstream Guards wrote[14] *The Art of Beating a Drum*. This was the first drum manual using staff notation. Two years later he produced *Potter's Drum, Flute and Bugle Duty Tutor*, which was accepted in 1817 as the universal standard to be used by the British Army. Samuel had also started selling drums and other musical instruments from a shop in Westminster, but he registered the business in his infant son's name 'Henry Potter and Co.' This was because as a regular soldier, Samuel could not do business with his employer (the Army). By the time Samuel Potter died, another son called George had founded an establishment at Aldershot. Both businesses were to sell military drums world wide – the most notable and durable product being the brass shell side drum.

The decoration or emblazoning of drum shells was another continental idea adopted by the British Army. The first record[15] of drums being emblazoned in the United Kingdom is a warrant to the Royal Regiment of Guards dated 1662. In the following century emblazoning started to become the norm and such drums took on an importance second only to a regiment's colours.

The origin of a regimental 'Corps of Drums' lies in the 'massing' together in one unit for ceremonial or military purposes, of the individual drummer/fifer/piper/bugler assigned as the signallers to the component companies of a regiment (as described on page 9). Massing of drummers and other musicians alongside the colours of British Army regiments in battle was first[16] seen during the Napoleonic wars. When *Potter's Drum, Flute and Bugle Duty Tutor* was published in 1812, it used the phrase 'Corps of Drums & Flutes'. Officially such a unit was not recognised until the Cardwell Army Reforms of 1872.

Initially 'drummer' was the designation of all in the corps of drums regardless of the instrument played, though multi-instrumentalism such as drummer/bugler and drummer/fifer was the common requirement of members in a corps of drums. This 'everyone's a drummer' concept suited those regiments with clandestine pipers (see page 8). When pipes were authorised for such regiments, its corps of drums was often initially re-designated 'The Massed Drums and Pipes' to reflect the seniority of the drums. Such a title is still used by the Gordon Highlanders to describe its pipe band rather than the commonly used 'Pipes and Drums'.

Bugles in the British Army

In the Middle Ages, the increasing use of gunpowder for artillery or muskets made a drum's battle field signals hard to discern and it started to be augmented or replaced. First by the buisine, the two metre long, straight trumpet of the period, then its shorter relation the trompe and then its diminutive version the trumpette. As with the drums before, an efficient means of signalling was achieved by a complex system of 'calls'.

Around 1750 a semi-circular copper horn from Germany started to replace the trompe. To improve ease of handling in the British Army, the length of the horn was 'wrapped around' once. In 1798 the first official book of British Army bugle calls was published[17].

By 1858, a second 'wrap' of tubing was added to the bugle, and this was known as the British Compact Design. Both the single and double wrap designs were valveless and could only play five or six notes of the natural horn. This was adequate for battlefield signalling but bore no comparison with the fife in reproducing marches and tunes.

However in 1810, a keyed bugle was invented and patented by Joseph Halliday, the Bandmaster of the Cavan Militia in Dublin. This keyed bugle or Royal Kent Bugle, gave a full chromatic scale of notes and enabled the instrument to play military marches.

Rifle Regiments evolved at much the same time as the start of the demise of the drum in battle. Consequently a corps of buglers (i.e. without drums) was therefore a feature of their ceremonial parades. Such 'Bugle Corps' often marched to the fore under the command of a Bugle-Major. It would appear that ceremonial 'Bugle Corps' existed as early as 1804 when a James Gilbert wrote a manual of calls for riflemen that also included thirty-six marches and quicksteps. These were written for three parts but include no drum part. Clearly these tunes were composed for ensemble playing by a corps of bugles.

Bugle Corps were officially authorised by the Cardwell Reforms of 1872, although most rifle regiments (including the London Irish Rifles) had, in reality, had them for some time.

See the conquering heroes come!
Sound the bugle, beat the drum!

(Second World War publicity photographs)

The Genealogy of Drums and Bugles in the London Irish Rifles

Like any organisation, a pipe band undergoes changes from time to time. However the frequency of change in the Drums and Bugles of the L.I.R. Pipe Band has been disproportionately high. This is understandable because the Band has its origins in three distinct traditions of the British Army. It should be remembered that:

- as a Regiment the L.I.R. has had a Regimental Military Band;
- as a Rifle Regiment it has had a Bugle Corps;
- as an Irish Regiment it has had its Pipes & Drums.

The impact of these three influences has waxed and waned over the years and it is nigh impossible to give a coherent description of how today's Drums and Bugles has evolved. For example there have been periods when:

1. The Pipe Band has been led by:
- a Bugle Major carrying a ceremonial cane,
- or a Drum Major carrying a ceremonial mace.

Bugle Major M. Mullhall,
who joined the L.I.R as a bugler in
1862, became Bugle Major in 1880
and served the Regiment for over
45 years.

2. The Pipe Band has paraded:
- with its buglers at the rear,
- with its buglers to the fore,
- or with no buglers at all.

3. The drummers have paraded 'wearing' bugles:
- purely as ornamentation,
- or to play as an integral part of the Band's performance.

4. The bass drummer wore:
- a leather apron,
- or a leopard skin.

Unfortunately the reasons behind these and other changes were never recorded. That they happened is obvious from photographs and published recollections. So the paragraphs that follow are an honest attempt, albeit written by two pipers, to briefly reflect the history of the Regiment's Drums and Bugles and how they have evolved to contribute to the phenomenon that is the Pipes & Drums of the London Irish Rifles.

The Drums and Bugles of the Early London Irish Rifles

As a rifle regiment, it is likely that the London Irish Rifles would have had buglers from the outset in 1859. Certainly it is recorded that Michael Mullhall joined the Regiment as Bugler in 1862 and in 1880 was promoted Bugle Major overseeing a bugle corps of some 30 buglers. B/M Mullhall served the Regiment for over 45 years and when marching at the head of the band was described[18] as "a terror to every bus on the line of route from Somerset House to Hyde Park, by reason of his dogged determination to have room for the London Irish at all costs".

The Regimental Band (formed 1861) would have included a snare drum and a bass drum but no record has been found of the composition of the Band prior to 1906 (see photograph on page 13). At that time the Regimental Band included two snare drums and a bass drum – all rope tensioned. The Bugle Corps of 1908 had shallow rod tension drums, as did the First World War Regimental Band (see photographs on pages 96 and 22 respectively).

L.I.R. Horizontal Bugler,
at the Annual Volunteer Forces' Rifle
Display on Wimbledon Common, 1875.

The L.I.R. Bugle Corps
and its drummers,
circa 1908.

Note: The white mustachioed B/M
Mullhall is in his 46th year with
the London Irish Rifles.

(photograph courtesy of Steve Spellwood,
The Corps of Drums Society.)

The Drums of the London Irish Rifles

The two L.I.R. Battalion Pipe Bands established for the First World War used Potter's 'Guard Pattern' brass side drums with green ropes and dark green lugs. Only the bass and tenor drums appear to have been emblazoned at that time. In fact there is no evidence of side drums carrying the regimental title, crest and battle honours until the 1950's.

During the 1950's proofed nylon drum heads were introduced for side drums and by the end of that decade a totally plastic head was in use. In tone they were not as good as skin but, being totally impervious to British rain, they were a significant advantage.

Rope tension drums were used throughout the first 50 years of the Pipe Band's existence. In spite of the use of full depth rod tension drums by military bands elsewhere in the world, they were rejected[19] by the British Army until the 1950's. Even after the acceptance of the inevitable by the War Department, British regiments were slow to take up the idea, though regimental pipe bands were quicker than most. The London Irish first had rod tension drums in 1964 whilst the Royal Marines held out until 1985.

In 1930, the Premier Drum Company had produced a full depth, rod-tensioned side drum suitable for pipe bands. A year later the Dalziel Highland Pipe Band won the World Championship using the new-fangled drums. Needless to say other competition bands adopted rod tension drums. The subsequent introduction of plastic batter heads, and then snares immediately under the batter heads, caused[20] "revolutionary advances in side drumming techniques". In part this was because these competition bands were not really marching bands in the army sense. Being relatively stationary they had more freedom to exploit unusual patterns and place accents and stresses in unusual positions. When the London Irish changed to rod tension side drums it embraced this style of drumming, which over a period of 30 years had become known as the 'Scots' style of pipe band beating.

Tea break at Pirbright, 1939.
Drummers are not always at the back of the Band.

96

The L.I.R. Drum Corps
and no sign of buglers, 1980.

The Bugles of the London Irish Rifles

When, in the early 1930s, Col. Mulholland told the Regimental Military Band that their services were no longer required (see page 29), he continued[21] that "any instruments were theirs to take away with the exception of the drums and bugles". He clearly intended to integrate the drums and bugles into the planned peacetime Regimental Pipe Band.

By the time the Regimental Pipe Band became a reality, the 'Drums' and 'Bugles' had been totally absorbed into what was called the Pipes & Drums of The London Irish Rifles. Effectively the Bugle Corps as such disappeared, though the Pipe band was to be led by a Bugle Major. Initially the drummers carried bugles (and some actually played them) and during the Second World War there were one or two stand alone buglers in the ranks. However by the time the Regimental Association took over responsibility for the Band in 1969, bugles were not even worn by the drummers for decorative purposes.

Spit and Polish!
Cleaning & maintenance is required to ensure a faultless performance.

This was to remain the case until 1992 when Roy 'Nobby' Clarke re-established the London Irish Bugle Corps with bugles borrowed from the R.I.R. Roy came to the L.I.R. with 15 years regular army service under his belt. He had been taught the bugle by the legendary Drum Major Bus of the Royal Gloucesters and had a complete understanding of what makes a traditional and successful military bugle corps. Roy researched the L.I.R. previous bugle corps – its uniform and calls. Training was organised at the R.I.R. Ballymena H.Q. Consequently the current-day London Irish Bugle Corps is pretty authentic even down to the wearing of envelope busbys for the first time in 50 years.

Nowadays high/low pitch bugles with slide are used so that they can be tuned to the pipe chanter.

The Bugle Major

If there were such a thing as a 'Text Book for Bugle Majors' it would say[22] that by tradition:

> The Bugle Major is the head of a band when on parade. Marching in front of the band, the Bugle Major is usually of imposing bearing, and his drill should always be flawless and his uniform immaculate. He is responsible for discipline and dress in the band (including the important role of marshalling the players at parades and performances), but his primary responsibility is to lead the band on parade by giving the drill commands. As it is difficult to be heard over a pipe band, the Bugle Major uses a combination of vocal commands and signals with the ceremonial cane he carries. The cane will be held in different positions to signify halts, marking time, wheels and the end of tunes.
>
> The Bugle Major has usually graduated to the position from the ranks of the drummers or buglers.

In its hundred year history, the Pipes & Drums of the London Irish Rifles have been led by many Bugle Majors (sometimes called Drum Majors – see page 127), who have more than satisfied the above criteria. Two Bugle Majors in particular were outstanding, and in their time were the public face of the Pipes & Drums of London Irish Rifles.

Bugle Major Bert Thackery

Bert Thackery was appointed Bugle Major in 1937 in what became known as Macnamara's Band. During the 1920s he had been a regular soldier with the Royal Scots – a regiment of such long-standing that its men called themselves 'Pontius Pilate's Bodyguard'. Bert was proud to be a 'Bodyguard' until an L.I.R piper from Ireland said "Well that explains the Crucifixion!" On leaving the army Bert played the side drum in the Great Western Railwayman's Pipe Band before joining the London Irish Rifles.

Though short in height (it was rumoured the Bugle Major's cane and sword had to be especially shortened for him), he was big in stature and imposed himself on the Band for nearly 25 years. It was no accident of alliteration that he was known as 'Tiger' Thackery.

He started the Second World War as the Regiment's Senior Bugle Major and helped in the establishment and training of the Young Soldiers Battalion. During the War Weapons Week of 1941, Bert had the honour of leading the Regiment's Massed Bands of the First, Second and 70th Young Soldiers Battalions on the only occasion they played together during the War (see page 43).

In 1942 he was transferred to the Royal Ulster Rifles. It was his proud boast that he was the only London Irish Rifleman who participated in the historic D-Day landings of June 1944 – the 2nd. Bn. R.U.R. being part of the 9th Infantry Brigade at Sword Beach, Normandy.

When the London Irish Rifles were reformed in 1947 and its Pipes & Drums resuscitated at an effective strength, Bert was back at the Duke of York's as the Bugle Major of his beloved Band. This was an appointment he held until he retired from the Band in 1960.

Bugle Major Roy Clarke who, calling on his vast knowledge of military musc and tradition, has revitalised the Bugle Corps of the London Irish Rifles since 1992.

Bugle Major Bert 'Tiger' Thackery. Short in height but big in stature. Was the cane and sword shortened to meet his requirements?

(TOP LEFT)
H.R.H. the Duke of Kent complains to B/M Smith that one tune from the Pipes & Drums of London Irish Rifles was quite insufficient[23] during the 1981 London T.A. Parade.

(TOP RIGHT)
London Pride Week, 1972. B/M Smith leads the L.I.R. contingent of the Massed Pipes and Drums past Edward Heath, the then British Prime Minister.

Bugle Major Gordon Smith

If Bert Thackery could be said to be short (and he was), Gordon Smith was certainly tall – 6 foot 4 inches tall.

Gordon was 13 years old when he joined the London Irish Cadets. He was drawn to the sound of the Pipes & Drums and soon joined the Band. He quickly became a proficient drummer and bugler under the tuition of Dennis Halsey. His first appearance with the L.I.R. Band in 1962 was as a tenor drummer but he was soon the Band's regular bass drummer.

In 1968, aged 22 he was appointed the Bugle Major in succession to John Furness. With the benefit of R.U.R training in Germany, he became everything a bugle major should be. His drill was flawless, his uniform immaculate, he maintained discipline and led the Band on parade with cool authority whilst all the time being one of the London Irish Lads.

London Irish Social events during the 70's at the Duke of York's were often enlivened by a performance from a mini show-band Gordon had originally formed with Paul 'Mickey' Finn, another L.I.R. drummer. However it was guitars, not drums, they played in 'The Silver Shamrocks'. Over the years the personnel of this band changed but Gordon remained the permanent feature. Other Pipe Band members involved at one stage or another were Don Wilson (guitar), John Plummer (drums), Sammy Moore (trumpet), David Murphy (drums) and Brian Smith (guitar/clarinet).

Gordon retired as the Band's Bugle Major in 1980 but came back to help out for a brief period after his successor Jim Powell retired in 1993.

An interesting foot note is that when Gordon Smith became the Band's Bugle Major, his place on the bass drum was temporarily taken by a young tenor drummer called Allan Dawes (*pictured left*). Nearly 40 years later Allan is a bass drummer of international repute. He has played with most of the world's top class pipe bands and is the bass drummer of choice when recording studios require such talent. Uniquely for bass drummers he receives full credit for his playing on the liner notes of the CDs he plays on.

Mike Crowley

When Andy Ridler's reign (seen as drum supremo) came to an end (see page 68), Mike Crowley took on the mantle of motivator and teacher to aspiring and established L.I.R. drummers. Thought to be a Scot through his membership of the King's Own Scottish Borderers (K.O.S.B.), he was in fact born in Fulham of predominantly Irish genealogy.

Mike had seen active service in Germany, Palestine and Korea. In this last conflict[24] he was badly wounded and as a consequence was 'invalided out' of the K.O.S.B. in 1952. In his six years service with the K.O.S.B., he had become an expert drummer and attained 'silver bugling status'. For the remainder of his life he used these skills to encourage and teach countless would-be drummers and buglers. Most notably he performed this role with the London Scottish for nearly 30 years.

However, during the 1970's and 1980's Mike was also with the London Irish Rifles – not only as the drum and bugle tutor but also regularly performing with the Band. His knowledge, experience and expertise significantly raised the standard of the corps of drums. Many of the L.I.R. youngsters Mike trained from scratch became championship standard drummers.

Mike was serious about his drumming but he was not a serious person. His good humour and sense of fun was legendary – even down to augmenting all the drummers' uniforms on one occasion with a badge proclaiming 'Drummers Rule. OK!'

Inspirational Mike Crowley, the drum & bugle tutor to the London Irish Rifles during the 1970's and 1980's.

References:

1. http://www.vsl.co.at/english/instruments/drums/drums/tenor_drum/History.htm
2. http://www.ajpropercussion.com/dc_hist.html
3. http://www.vsl.co.at/english/instruments/drums/drums/tenor_drum/History.htm
4. http://www.windsor.k12.co.us/wms/mperry/Hist%20Perc.htm
5. *The Drum* by Hugh Barty-King published The Royal Tournament 1988; page 118.
6. http://archiver.rootsweb.com/th/read/BOER-WAR/2001-06/0991892338.
7. http://www.vsl.co.at/english/instruments/drums/drums/bass_drum/History.htm
8. http://www.scottniven.co.uk/drumming/interviews/articles/evolution.html
9. op. cit. Hugh Barty-King; page 89.
10. http://:www.hpb.dk/artikler/gb/Young_and_Chatto-History_of_the_military_drum.pdf
11. http://www.musicweb.uk.net/classrev/2002/ Dec02/drums.htm
12. http://www.musicweb.uk.net/classrev/2002/Dec02/drums.htm
13. www.corpsofdrums.com/history.htm
14. http://www.canadianstandard.ca/wtsi/hist.html & http://www.mcgee-flutes.com/henry_potter.htm
15. op. cit. Hugh Barty-King; page 27.
16. op. cit. Hugh Barty-King; page 80.
17. www.guardian.co.uk/military/story/ 0,11816,1049553,00.html
18. *The London Irish Rifles Magazine* 1894
19. op. cit. Hugh Barty-King; page 118.
20. W.G.F. Boag in the May 1974 *Bulletin of the Military Historical Society*: page 160.
21. *The Regimental Centenary* published by the London Irish Rifles Regimental Association, 1959; page 62.
22. based on www.wspd.wellington.net.nz/pipebands/drummajor.htm
23. *The Emerald* No.38; page 18.
24. *The London Scottish Gazette*; No.1048.

Band Members Past and Present

Many musicians have contributed to the success of the Pipes & Drums of the London Irish Rifles over the past 100 years and these are listed overleaf. Performing membership dates are given where known. Every effort has been made to ensure the accuracy of this list and any omissions or corrections should be notified to the Secretary of the Regimental Association (see page 114).

The Pipes & Drums of the London Irish Rifles.

1	1st., 2nd. and Young Soldiers Bns.	1941
2	Near the Front	1916
3	The Cenotaph	1970
4	Loos Sunday	1986
5	St. Patrick's Sunday	1998

Pipers
* denotes Pipe Major
at some stage

Aarons, Sam 1914--19
Alsop, Stan 1939-43
Arlow, Patrick 1944-48
Aspinall, William 2005-present
Barnard, John 1970's
Barr, Judy 2000
Beck 1939-46
Bewshear, Mick 1960's/70's
*Blackwell 1930's
Brightman, Tom 1939-45
*Brown, George, 1940-45
Brown, Joe 1990's
Brown, 'Mo' 1939-42
Burns, Michael 1946-48
Burt, Chris 1970-95
Button, Len 1970's & 80's
Callaghan, Tom 1950-60
Carr, Ted 1930-1960
Carvell Andy 1914-18
*Clancey, Con 1914-18
Clare, Tom 1939-46
Coffee, Charlie 1940's
Conway, Tom 1915-18
Cotter, J 1914-18
Corkesh, 1914-18
Cornish, Bob 1960-75
Dempsey, Frank 1960-76
Diamond, Hughie 1970-96
Dennis, T 1950's
Dennis, B 1950's
Doyle, Sean 1976-84
Doughty, Pete 2004-present
Dowling, Frank 1970's & 80's
Dullaghan, Jim 1970's & 80's
*Evans, Archie 1933-63
Fallis, John 1994-98
Farrell, Joe 1972-86
Finn, Colin 1970's
Flook, Brian 1990's
Fogarty, Michael 1932-35
Fogarty, Paddy 'Pa' 1914-19, 1932-35
Fogarty, Patrick 1930-35
Fox, Breda 1980's
*Franklin, Johnny 1928-85
Franklin, Len 1937-43
Gardender, 1914-18
Gerary, George 1960's
Gibbons E.E 1914-18
Grant, Pat 1970-2000

Goodman, Terry 1997 - present
Hall, Peter 1986 - present
Henning, F.S."Mick" 1932-42
Horder, Peter 1940-46
Hough, Frank 1914-18
Hough, Harry 1914-18
Hughes 1940-46
Hughes Bertie 1942-45
Hutchins, Len 1940-60
*Jackson 1939-46
Jefferies, 'Jeff' 1943-46
Jelly, Tom 1980's
Judd, Charlie 1932-39
Kavanagh 1950's
Kelly, Sean 1970's
Kerney, Adrian 1993-2001
Kennedy, 1914-18
Kerr, Patsy 1942-'44
Kydd, Burt 'Captain' 1980's
Kimber, Ronnie 1940-46
King, Gerry 1967-84
King, Terry 1967-84
Learmonth, 1939-45
Lehmann,'Mick'1939-45
Links, Maurice 1997-2001
Littlejohn, A 1930's
Littlejohn B 1930's
Lorhick, Bert 1960's
Lowrey, P 1939-44
Luckman, Eric 1972-76
MacDonald 1946-48
Mackesy, Roy 'Cowboy' 1939-46
*Maloney, John 1908-20
Maguire, Michael 1980's
Maher, Mick
Marshal, Dick 1914-19
Marra, Tom
Mason, Philip 2000-present
McCombie, James 1990-2003
McConnel, Bill 1970's
McGrath, Helen 1980's
McManus 1941-45
McMaster, Archie 1970-present
McKenna, Sean 1940-44
McMullen, Billy 1960's-90's
Mead, Ray 1939-42
Melia, John 1960's
Melia, Mick 1939-42
Messerchmitt, John 1960's
Milne, Timmy 1939-45
*Miller, Jim
Modlock, Bill 1974-77
Morris, J 1990's
Mulqueen, Dennis 1939-43

*Murphy, Dominic 1982-2003
Murphy, Joe 1980-99
Murphy, Seamus 1980s
Newcombe, George
   'Piper 'F' 1936-46
*Nicholson, Allan 1939-42
*Nicholson, George 1940-42, 1959-70
Nolan, Martin 1990 - present
Nolan, Mick 1939-45
*O'Brien, Pat 1939-98
O'Brien, Joe 1946-49
O'Callaghan, 'Sandy' 1930-95
O'Callaghan, Tom 1939
O'Connor, Kevin1960's
O'Donnel, Bernie 1960's/70's
O'Malley, Mick 1973-95
*O'Sullivan, Kevin 1938-50
Purvis, Dave 1964-2001
Raun, 1914-19
Reeves, Bernie 1970's
Riley, George 1940-46
Riley, Jim 1960's
Rostant, Louisa 1997-2001
Rostant, Joanna 1997-2001
Sands, Pat 199-present
Savage, Alf 1939-42
Shanahan, Brian guest piper
Shanahan, Eddie 1933-37
Shanahan, Jackie 1938-1948
Shanahan, Michael guest piper
*Shanahan, Sean 1988 - 2004
Shanahan, Arthur 'Toddy' 1938-42
Shield, 'Jock' 1939-42
Smith, Brian 1966-present
Stanton, Colin 1940-45
Stevens, Phil 1970's
*Starck, Albert 1907-18
Stranix, Johnny 1970's
Stumpo, Ben 1990's
Sullivan, Pat 1960-73
Tannel, Louis 1950's
Tucker, Dave 1980's & 90's
Turner 1939-45
*Vaughan, Michael 1964-present
*Wallace, Jim 'Cookie' 1962-72
Wallace, Heather 2001-present
Wicks, 1940-41
Williams, Taffy 1941-46
Wilkie, Bruce 1980's
Willis, George 1939-49, 1977-2001
Willis, Leslie 1940-45
Wilson, Alex 2005-present
Woodley, Phil 1939-45
Woods, Harry 1914-39

Drummers & Buglers
** denotes Drum Major
*** denotes Bugle Major
+ denotes Dog Major
or Dog Handler

Baines, Dickie 1939-42
Batey, Redford 1970's
Barnard, Jim 1959-79
Barnett 1940-45
Burns, Ken 'Smokey Joe' 1939-46
Buttons, 1935-43
Carter, H 1910-18
Cavan 1940-45
Childs, 1939-45
***Chubb, Maurice 1939-46
***Clarke, Roy 'Nobby' 1991-present
Clarke, Jim
Clarke. Lynn 1980's
Clarke, Maureen 1980's
Coles, D 1914-18
Cook, 1940's
Craig, Austin 1960's
Course, Phil 1980s
Crowley, Mick 1982-92
Deacon, Peter
Dempsey, Sean 1979-95,
          2004-present
Dawes, Allan 1960's
+Downard, Alex 1999-2001
Downer, Bill 'Snouter' 1935-42
Downer, 'Governor' 1939-45
Duncan, E 1914-18
Dunkley, Joseph 1946-48
Dutriet, A 1914-18
Elliot, J 1914-18
+Evans, Norman 1950's
Faronfield, J 1914-18
Finn, Paul 'Mickey' 1970's
Forest, Dominic 1970's
Foulis, Dave
***Furness, John 1962-71
Foley, J 1914-18
Gibson 1914-19
Goldsmith, Joe 1939-45 1947-50
Goulding 'Pluto' 1939-42
Gibbons, George 1970's
Goodbear, J 1914-19
***Groves, Mick 1939-50
Hambleton, Richard 1980's
Harbarrow, E 1914-19
+Halsey, Dennis 1960's & '70's
Harrington 1940-45
Harris 1914-19

Harris, John 1960's & 70's
Hartley, Kevin 1970's
Hawksley, Rochelle 2004-present
Henchey, Don 2000-present
Homes, E 1914-19
House, R 1914-19
Hunt 1940-45
Jackson, Bill 1937-80
Jackson, George 1934-40
+Jackson, George 1940-45
Kelly, Steve 1970's & 80's
Kelly, Terry 1970's & 80's
King, Barry 1980-94
King, George 1937-39
Klien, Albie 1940-50
Leggatt 1940-45
Links, Maurice 1997-2001
MacKay 1946-48
Mason, Avril 2000 to present
Mason, Oliver 2000 to present
Mayle, Bert 1950's
McCarthy, Tim 1940-46,1980's
McCartney, Sam 'Scrumsie' 1960's
**McDonagh, Brendan 1991-2000
McGeary, Ron 1969-73
McMullen, John 1980s
**Metcalf, Tom 2000-03
***Metcalf 1942-46
Miller, Richard 1970's
Moore, Sammy 1966-70
Mullins, 'Sailor' 1939-41
Mulqueen, Dennis 1970-2001
Murphy, David 1977-87

O'Connor, Pat 1980's
O'Connell Lee 1980's
O'Donnal, Mick 1960's
O'Leary, John 1920's & 1930's
O'Neil, H 1914-19
Pender, G 1988
Plummer John 1970-2000
***Powell, Jim 1970-93
Powell, Mike 1970-74
Powell, Tim 1980's
&*Raper, Tom 2000-present
Ridler, Andy 1951-79
Riley, Harry 'Rasher' 1941-46
Riley, Michael 1980's
Robinson, Eric 1941-45
+Roberts, Alan
Rogers, Paul 1980's
Russell, Bob 1960's & 1970's
***Scarborough, A 1960's
Shannon, Ted 1960's
+Sheridan, Les 1986-present
***Smith, Gordon 1962-1980, 1993
Smith, Michael 1994-present
Stillwood, G 1914-19
Stumpo, Ben 1990's
Sturgeon, Bob 1970's
Sullivan, C 1914-19
Swain 1941-42
Sweeney, Francis 1939-45
***Thackery, Bert 'Tiger 1937-60
Taylor, Charlie 1939-41
Taylor, Ernie 1939-41
***Taylor, Fred 1939-45
Threadgold, E 1914-19
Turner, A 1914-19
Vaughan, Catherine 1997-2000
+Varga, Mark 1997-present
Wallace, Bob 2000-present
Wallace, Sue 2001-present
Ware 1940-45
Warren, Terry 'Bunny' 1960's & 70's
Watts, Gary 2003-present
Welding, Ted 1997-present
Wilson, Don 1970's & 80's
Wood H 1914-19

**Pipe Major Albert Starck
and Drummer Carter.**
Albert was not only the first Pipe Major
of the London Irish, Rifles, but was also
the principal bagpipe maker for the
British Army.

(from the *Regimental Magazine* 6 May 1911.)

103

Family Ties and Dynasties

Over the years brothers or sisters have played together, father and son(s) have marched together or one generation has followed in the footsteps of another. Sometimes the link is not obvious by the surname. The following are examples of family ties in the London Irish Rifles' Pipe Band.

The Houghs

Frank and Harry Hough were piping brothers with the regiment during the First World War. They survived action at Loos, the Somme and Ypres. After the war they were founder members of the Tottenham Irish Pipe Band and taught many of the bandsmen who formed the basis of the L.I.R.'s. 1939-45 Pipe Bands. Expert pipers, both brothers also judged piping competitions.

The Fogartys

Paddy Fogarty learned his piping at the Borough Pipe Band. On the outbreak of the First World War, he joined the Queen's Own Regiment. Although this regiment had no pipe band, in his spare moments he practised his pipes in a nearby field. On the last such occasion, a mounted officer jumped over the boundary hedge for an explanation. The next day, against his wishes, Paddy was transferred to the L.I.R. Assigned to the 2nd. Bn. Band, he served in France, Macedonia and Egypt. Ironically he was the only soldier listed as a 'piper' in the L.I.R.'s 1914-19 nominal roll of some 9,500 men.

After the First World War, Paddy founded the Tottenham Irish Pipe Band but also played intermittently with the L.I.R. After the Second World war he founded the Tower Hill Pipe Band with whom he played until he was well into his eighties. Paddy's lasting legacy is the numerous Irish tunes he set for the pipes - including the jigs entitled: 'The Leg of the Duck', 'Geese in the Bog' and 'Hot Potcheen'.

Paddy's children were excellent pipers too, especially Michael who was the British Junior Champion and the 1930's saw Paddy and sons Michael and Patrick all piping with the L.I.R.. Paddy's daughter and granddaughter, both named Sheila, regularly practised with the London Irish in the 1970's although they never paraded with the Band.

The Nicholsons

Allan Nicholson was already a 'time served soldier' when he volunteered for the L.I.R. in 1939. Although an accomplished piper, he was recognised as a world class bass drummer who would play the drum in a band provided its drummers wore kilts. However in 1931 he was to 'guest' as the L.I.R.'s bass drummer, wearing trousers, when the Regiment visited Ulster.

As an experienced soldier, piper and drummer Allan was appointed the Pipe Major to the L.I.R. Young Soldiers Battalion to help train their Band. Already in his forties, he was declared medically unfit in 1943. After the War he played with the Tower Hill Band and lived to the ripe old age of 94.

Allan Nicholson's son Ailein Nicholson (known as George) enrolled as a piper in the Royal Irish Fusiliers at the earliest opportunity. However, on the outbreak of war, his father claimed him back for the L.I.R. to serve in the Young Soldiers Battalion. On reaching operational military age he was transferred to the Seaforth

Paddy 'Pa' Fogarty, 1915.
The start of a piping dynasty at the London Irish and the driving force of many an Irish pipe band in London.

(ABOVE)
P/M Allan Nicholson, 1942.

(BELOW)
P/M George Nicholson, 1965
son of Allan Nicholson.

Michael Fogarty, 1936.

Highlanders. Here he was a regular soldier until 1959 when he rejoined the L.I.R. In 1965 he was appointed Pipe Major of the L.I.R. Band but his tenure was short lived and he returned to the ranks.

His piping hindered by arthritis in his hands, George's later years were spent compiling the three volume collection of his own compositions which nowadays are often used by competition bands. Notable amongst his compositions is the slow air 'The Dreams of Old Pa Fogarty'.

The Vaughans

Michael Vaughan's 40 years continuous service with the Band is a record unlikely to be broken – particularly as it is still increasing!

A grandson of the legendary Paddy Fogarty he was piping from an early age. By the time he joined the L.I.R. in 1964, he had been tutored at the Tower Hill Pipe Band not only by Grandpa Paddy but also by his Uncle Micky and his father Johnny Vaughan, an accomplished piper and musician who had married Paddy's daughter Kathleen.

When Pat O'Brien (see page 71) stepped down as Pipe Major of the L.I.R. Pipe Band in 1986, Michael was his natural successor. Under his leadership the Band continued to go from strength to strength. After what he has described as "ten long eventful years" he gave up the appointment of Pipe Major in 1997. However he continues to be a stalwart of the Band, deputising for the Pipe Major when required.

Micky, as he has always been called by the Band, is highly regarded not only for his musicianship and knowledge, but also for the support, encouragement, and most importantly the friendship he has proffered to all over the decades.

Michael's daughter Catherine became the fourth generation of the Fogarty line to play with the Band when she performed as a drummer with the L.I.R. from 1997 to 2000. Subsequently she has seen active service in the Territorial Army with the Royal Logistic Corps in the Iraq Conflict.

(RIGHT)
P/M Michael Vaughan,
whose 40 years service with the Pipes & Drums of the London Irish Rifles has rarely been surpassed.

(FAR RIGHT)
Catherine Vaughan,
the latest in a long line of 'Pa' Fogarty's descendants to play for the Pipe Band.

The Murphys

As a teenager in the 1930's, Joe Murphy was another piper who was taught the pipes by Paddy Fogarty at the Tottenham Pipe Band. An early conscript to the British Eighth Army, Joe was captured in Egypt in 1942 and was a P.O.W. for the next three years. In the prison camp he practised endlessly on a set of pipes loaned to him by an Australian P.O.W and by the end of the war he was a highly proficient piper. In 1980 Joe brought his piping talents to the London Irish Pipe Band and was joined soon thereafter by his son-in-law Dave Tucker.

Another piper to join the London Irish during the 1980's was Joe's nephew Dominic Murphy. Following a meteoric rise through the ranks, Dominic was appointed the L.I.R. Pipe Major in 1997 and soon stamped his personality on the Band. In 2002 he was the first London Irishman to be appointed the Pipe Major of the London Regiment.

The Shanahans

Three generations of Shanahans have played pipes for the London Irish Rifles. It started with Eddie who, having learned the pipes with the Tottenham Irish, honed his technique with the Dagenham Town Irish Pipe Band. He served as a territorial in the L.I.R Band from 1933 to 1937. From 1939-46 he was a piper with the Royal Scottish Fusiliers but after the War he rejoined the London Irish Band.

Eddie's youngest brother Jackie enrolled in the L.I.R. as a lad and so impressed the Band's tutor, Mr Bob Hill, previously of the Argyll & Sutherland Highlanders, that in 1938 he recommended Jackie to his former regiment.

Toddy, the middle brother, joined the L.I.R. from the Dagenham Band in 1938 and was with the 1st. Bn. until 1942 when he was appointed Pipe Major to the 8th Bn of the R.U.R. Prior to this, on the outbreak of war, he had 'claimed back' Jackie from the Argylls for the London Irish. Jackie was to remain with the 1st. Bn. L.I.R. for the duration of the Second World War.

(ABOVE)
Piper Joe Murphy, 1987,
who for the last 19 years of his piping career played with the L.I.R. Pipe Band.

(BELOW)
P/M Dominic Murphy,
the first London Irishman to be appointed Pipe Major of the London Regiment, 2002.

The Shanahan Pipers.

(THIS PAGE, LEFT TO RIGHT)
Eddie Shanahan, 1960.
P/M Toddy Shanahan, 1938.
P/M Jackie Shanahan, 1940.

(OPPOSITE PAGE, LEFT TO RIGHT)
Brian Shanahan, 1958.
Michael Shanahan, 1970.
P/M Sean Shanahan, 2000.

Sgt. Daniel Shanahan, shown here in Bosnia with the R.E.M.E., has yet to follow the family tradition and play with the London Irish Rifles Pipe Band.

After the War, as Pipe Major of the 'Rimini Remnants' (see page 62), Jackie helped form the R.U.R.'s first peacetime pipe band (see page 63).

Brian and Michael Shanahan were two of the offspring of Eddie's marriage to Anna Nicholson, a daughter of Allan Nicholson (see page 104). Brian initially learned the pipes from his Dad before joining the L.I.R. Cadets where his grandfather, Allan Nicholson, was the piping tutor. He was also a member of Paddy Fogarty's Tower Hill Pipers before becoming Pipe Major of the London Scottish Cadet Band. He then joined the Royal Inniskilling Fusiliers as a regular soldier. Here he easily adjusted to the keyed chanter of the 'Brian Boru' pipes then still being used by the 'Skins', and was soon appointed a piping instructor for both the Highland Pipes and 'Brian Boru' Pipes at the North Irish Brigade's Piping School. After the army he played with a number of pipe bands including that of the London Irish Rifles with whom he still periodically performs playing his Uncle Jackie's pipes.

Michael's piping skills were acquired as a boy soldier with the Queen's Own Highlanders but it was the Royal Inniskilling Fusiliers that he chose to join as a regular soldier. He, like his brother, easily adjusted to the 'Brian Boru' chanter and was soon playing in the Regimental Pipe Band. When the 'Skins' were amalgamated into the new Royal Irish Rangers, they had to abandon their use of the 'Brian Boru' pipes and Michael's lasting claim to fame is that he was the last British Army piper to play 'Brian Boru' pipes. Nowadays he plays for the Regimental Association of the Royal Irish Rangers but makes 'guest appearances' from time to time with the L.I.R. Band wearing his R.I.R. uniform. Michael's son Daniel is also a piper.

Sean Shanahan learned the pipes from his father Brian. At the earliest opportunity Sean joined the local T.A. After ten years service with the Wiltshire Yeomanry, the pull of the Shanahan's spiritual home became too great and he transferred to the L.I.R to serve both as a soldier and piper. He is still active in both facets of the L.I.R. In 2003 he was temporarily appointed Pipe Major of the Pipes and Drums, and also saw service during the Iraq Conflict as a member of the multi-badged Tactical Air Control Party in Basra.

The Powells, the Kellys and the Rileys

Jim Powell joined the L.I.R. Band in 1976 as a bass drummer and deputy Bugle Major to Gordon Smith (see page 99). By 1980 Jim was the substantive Bugle Major and was to lead the band on many historic occasions.

Before joining the L.I.R. Jim had been with the Borough Pipe Band since 1947, first as a drummer then as its Drum Major. It was here that his elder son Micky learned drumming before joining the L.I.R. in 1972. After two years, Micky moved to the London Scottish where he remained until 2003 serving as its Drum Major for more than ten years. On several occasions father and son were to be seen side by side as the Massed Bands of the London Irish and London Scottish paraded.

Jim's younger son Tim learned his drumming at the London Scottish before moving to the Pride of Murray Pipe Band. However, he regularly turned out for the L.I.R. Band during the 1980's. At one stage during this period the L.I.R. Corps of Drums boasted three cousins; namely Tim Powell, Michael Riley and Steve Kelly. Steve and Michael had started at the Borough Pipe Band before joining the L.I.R. in their early teens. In their later drumming careers, Michael was the Grade 2 British Champion and Steve the Grade 3 World Champion.

Both Michael Riley and Steve Kelly were from drumming families. Michael's father Pat Riley played for the Borough Pipe Band whilst Steve's father Terry Kelly, having started at the Borough, was recruited in 1970 as the permanent bass drumming replacement for Gordon Smith (see page 99). Terry was to be the beating pulse for the L.I.R. Pipes & Drums for the next ten years.

(TOP LEFT)
Father & Son.
Jim & Micky Powell, respectively Bugle Major & Drum Major of the London Irish Rifles and the London Scottish, 1993.
(photo: Sharon Baseley, *Potters Bar Times*.)

(TOP RIGHT, LEFT TO RIGHT)
Drumming Cousins.
Tim Powell, Steve Kelly and Michael Riley, 1984.

(ABOVE)
Bass drummer Terry Kelly, 1972.

The Masons

Unique in the annals of the Band's history are Avril Mason and her two teenage sons Oliver and Philip. The family's involvement with the London Irish Rifles started when Philip saw a pipe band perform at first hand. He decided there and then he wanted to learn the pipes and promptly joined the London Irish as a trainee piper in 1998. He was followed by his brother Oliver in 2000 and mother Avril soon thereafter.

Nowadays they are established members of the Band. Avril is a tenor/bass drummer, Philip a piper Corporal and Oliver the Band's leading tipper – the ultimate mini-band! Although at over six foot each and still growing there is nothing 'mini' about the boys.

The Kings

Twins Gerry and Terry King were in their twenties before they learned to play the pipes with the Tower Hill Pipe Band. Here they were taught by their uncle Tom Nolan (whose brother Mick Nolan had been a piper in the 1st. Bn. L.I.R. Pipe Band throughout the Second World War). The Twins joined the Pipes & Drums of the London Irish Rifles in 1966 and were soon nicknamed 'the Bookends'. Gerry and Terry were to be very active members of the Band until 1984.

Drummer Barry King was taken to Friday night band practice as a toddler by his parents Gerry and Vera. He soon had drum sticks in his hands – courtesy of Andy Ridler (see page 68) and from an early age Barry was an unofficial London Irish drummer. He was allowed formally to join his father and uncle in the Band in 1980. He was just 13 years old and was to remain a permanent feature of the Drum Corps until he was 27. (He also features in the photograph on page 80.)

(TOP RIGHT)
The Mason Family.
Oliver, Avril and Philip; mother and sons in the 2004 Band.

(TOP LEFT)
The Piping King Twins.
Gerry & Terry King a.k.a. 'The Bookends' in the 1970s &1980's Band.

(ABOVE)
Barry King,
Gerry's drummer son, 1987.

The Rostant Sisters

Since the Regimental Association took control of the Band in 1969 membership has been open to all irrespective of gender or age.

Of note in the first category were Johanna and Louisa Rostant. These sisters started in Agnes O'Connel's London Irish Girl Pipers. Here Louisa learned the drums and Johanna learned the pipes under the tutelage of ex-P/M Crabbe. Later, whilst with the London Ambulance Service Pipe Band, Louisa also learned the pipes. They brought their skills to the London Irish in 1996 and were stalwarts for the next three years, performing with the Band both at the Royal Tournament and Nova Scotia International Tattoo (see pages 82 to 84).

Nowadays the sisters perform, wearing saffron kilts, in their own band known as the 'Castle Pipers'. Here the Pipe Major is Johanna who, as a solo piper, has performed at the Royal Albert Hall and the Royal Festival Hall. The sisters also have strong connections with the Somme Battlefield Pipe Band but have still been known to turn out for the L.I.R. in times of need.

The Smiths

Its not always the case that people called Smith are related but in the London Irish Rifles the exception proves the rule.

As a member of the L.I.R. Cadets, Brian Smith was drawn to the sound of the Pipes. Under the tuition of P/M Pat O'Brien (see page 71) he became a regular piper in the Band. Having mastered the pipes he took up the clarinet at evening classes and played this instrument and the guitar in the 'Silver Shamrocks' mini show band (see page 99). From the mid sixties onward he has been more or less a regular member of the Band and in 2004 was appointed the Pipe Major.

Another young starter with the Band was Brian's son Michael Smith, who joined when he was just 15 years old. Initially his drum tutor was Mike Crowley (see page 100) and to this day Michael is appreciative of the skills Mike passed onto him.

(ABOVE LEFT)
Piping Sisters.
The talented musicians Louisa and Johanna Rostant whose skills graced the L.I.R Band during the late 1990's.

(ABOVE RIGHT)
Father and Son.
P/M Brian Smith has been a regular in the Band since the 1960's and for the last decade has been joined by his drummer son Michael.

(ABOVE LEFT AND CENTRE)
Keeping it in the Family.
Drummer Jim (1959) & piper John (1972) Barnard are direct descendants of R.S.M. Fred Barnard.

(ABOVE RIGHT)
Daughter & Mother.
Heather & Sue Wallace, who are both members of the current Band.

(BELOW)
Royal Military School of Music Student.
Rochelle Hawksley is also a 2004 Band member.

The Barnards

Tenor drummer Jim Barnard was a son of Sergeant Major Fred Barnard (Second World War 1st. Bn. L.I.R.). Having originally joined the Band in 1959, Jim brought the modern style of beating and swinging from the Pride of Murray Pipe Band to the London Irish in the 1960's via the Deptford Irish Band where he had adapted the technique to the Irish repertoire. As a supplier of military band equipment and accessories he helped re-equip the Band when the Regimental Association assumed responsibility for its management. After leaving the Band in 1980 he played with the London Scottish.

John Barnard, a grandson of Fred (and a nephew of Jim) learned the pipes at the Deptford Irish Band from the age of ten. He joined the L.I.R. Cadets at the earliest opportunity and was admitted to the L.I.R. Band aged 13. For a time he carried the 'youngest piper's banner' and continued to perform with the Band for six further years after he joined the Regiment as a Territorial.

The Wallaces

Heather Wallace joined the L.I.R. Band in 2001 to satisfy her ambition to play the pipes. Her mother Sue, a brass player since she was 17 years old, also joined as a bugler. Both are now established Band members.

Heather studied the flute and piccolo at the Royal Military School of Music (R.M.S.M.) Kneller Hall before being assigned to the staff band of the Royal Signals in 2005. Here her first posting will be as a solo piper in the Falklands. Prior to the R.M.S.M., Heather was on a T.A. posting for the Royal Scots & Highlanders with the NATO led stabilisation force in Bosnia. Uniquely, she wore a medical corps belt and the L.I.R. piper's caubeen.. This reflected her duties as a combat medical technician and a company piper.

Royal Military School of Music Connections

Another Band member at the R.M.S.M in 2004 was L.I.R. bugler Rochelle Hawksley who was studying the clarinet.

(LEFT)
The 'Three Brothers'.
Stan Alsop, Harry and George Riley, 1940.

(BELOW)
Father & Son-in-Law.
65 years after first playing with the L.I.R., George Riley wishes his son-in-law Pete Doughty good luck for his first performance with the Band in 2004.

The Rileys, Stan Alsop and Pete Doughty

Harry Riley joined the First Battalion of the London Irish Rifles in 1939 at the same time as fellow Londoner Stan Alsop. Both soon enrolled in the Band as trainee musicians – Stan as a piper and Harry as a drummer. When his brother George was called up, Harry claimed him for the London Irish Rifles and he joined the band as a trainee piper. For the remainder of the war the three of them were inseparable and many thought all three were brothers. After the war, even when Stan emigrated to Canada in 1953, the three kept in touch. When Stan returned to Blighty in 1972, face to face links were established once again.

Harry died in 1995 but George and Stan are still in touch to this day – some 60 years after the end of the Second World War.

George Riley's son-in-law Pete Doughty did not start to learn to play the pipes until he was 54 years old. Then, like most late comers to a hobby, it became an all embracing passion. His daily early morning piping practice in a park near his home became the source of local bewilderment and the 'Phantom Piper' was sought by the local media.

Having mastered the basics with the tutor of the Deptford Irish Pipe Band he joined the Pipes & Drums of the London Irish Rifles in 2004.

Another connection Pete has with the London Irish Rifles is that his grandfather, Charles Thomas Doughty, was a sergeant in the London Irish Rifles during the First World War.

(LEFT)
Piper George Willis,
with his wife Rose and son George
P. Willis, 1949.

(RIGHT)
Piper Eric Luckman,
one of many pipers who initially
received encouragement from his
Uncle George Willis.

Willis and Luckman

Another to join the London Irish Rifles in the summer of 1939 was George Willis. Although not 20 years of age at the time, he had already been playing the pipes for nearly ten years. He had been taught by Allan Nicholson (see page 104) at the Tottenham Irish Band and had subsequently played with the Dagenham Town Irish and the Great Western Railwaymen's Pipe Bands.

By the outbreak of war he was an established piper with the London Irish Rifles. Soon appointed the Company Piper for 'D' Coy. 1st. Bn., he carried the pipe banner of the Dublin Fusiliers (motto 'fight like tigers and like elephants never forget'). His fighting days were brought abruptly to an end in early 1944 when he was captured at Anzio. After being repatriated at the end of the war (see page 57), he played with the immediate post war London Irish Band for a couple of years.

In 1955 George formed The Deptford Irish Pipe Band for youngsters in that area of South East London. Fifty years later the nucleus of that 'youth band' still plays together. In the early 1990's he helped revitalise the Borough Pipe Band in time for its Centenary in 1992.

Meanwhile in the 1970's, he had been enticed back to the L.I.R. Pipe Band by his old school friend Pat O'Brien who was now its Pipe Major. For the next 25 years George was again to play with L.I.R. Band. Nowadays, with George in his mid eighties, his piping activity is limited to imparting his knowledge to others and particularly teaching beginners the instrument.

George's enthusiasm for Irish music and pipe bands can be infectious and many of his relatives and friends caught the pipe band bug from him. Amongst these are his tenor drummer wife Rose, drum major daughter Kathleen, piper son George P. Willis (with whom he wrote this book) and nephew Eric Luckman.

Eric learned the pipes whilst he was a boy soldier in the REME and had further tuition whilst a regular soldier with the Royal Scots Greys. After eleven years service he left the Army in 1972 and promptly joined the Pipes & Drums of the London Irish Rifles. After four years playing with the L.I.R. he subsequently played with the Knightsbridge and Blue Bonnets Pipe Bands. A trained paramedic employed by the London Ambulance Service, he joined its pipe band in 1987 and still occasionally plays with them.

Association Band Presidents

When the Association took control of the Band in 1969 (see page 67 onwards), the MoD required that if the Band was to function as a Military Band in support of London Irish Rifles, it should continue to be managed by a responsible and reliable Band President. This task has been shouldered by the five Association Band Presidents since 1969. They have recruited the musicians, ensured their training and equipping, managed the finances, negotiated engagements and ensured the Band's ongoing viability.

Presidents of the Association's Pipe Band.

(TOP ROW, LEFT TO RIGHT)
Major Rodney Cockburn M.B.E.
1969-1985
Major John Fallis T.D.
1985-1994
Major Jim MacLeod
1994-1999 & 2003 - present

(BOTTOM ROW, LEFT TO RIGHT)
Major Rupert Wirgman T.D.
1999-2002
Major David Mogg T.D.
2002-2003

References:

Every effort has been made to ensure the accuracy of the personal information detailed in this chapter. Past and present band members have been interviewed, as have the relatives of those no longer with us.

The lists at pages 102 and 103 were compiled from many sources – none of which are comprehensive. Consequently corrections will be required. To keep the Museum's computerised master copy of this book up to date, omissions and corrections should be notified to:

The Secretary of the Regimental Association,
The London Irish Rifles,
c/o Connaught House,
4 Flodden Road, London SE5 9LL.

Regimental Mascots

The Irish Wolfhound Mascot of the London Irish Rifles, 1916.

(Reproduced under licence from ITN British Pathé.)

It is often said that the British is a nation of animal lovers and if its armed services are anything to go by this is certainly true. Animals of all descriptions have been adopted as official pets or regimental mascots.

For the first 40 years of his 160 years life, Timmy the Tortoise saw service on a succession of Royal Naval vessels until given a life ashore in 1892. The RAF appear to have a penchant for goats and dogs, whilst the Army have in their time adopted as mascots a veritable zoo – including a ferret held on the strength[1] of 1st. Bn. Prince of Wales's Own (as at Jan 2002).

Often the mascot 'marches' with the regimental band. Even after death, many are retained as talismen – stuffed and exhibited in the regimental museum.

The mascot of choice for Irish Regiments is the Irish wolfhound.

Irish Wolfhounds

The Irish wolfhound has been the National Dog of Ireland[2] for over 2,000 years. However the modern breed of Wolfhounds only dates from the 1880's. Their ancestors were originally called the Cu, a massive shaggy-coated dog used for hunting. They were thought[3] to have been brought to Ireland by the Celts sometime between 2500 B.C. and 1500 B.C. Standing on its hind legs, the Cu could reach up to seven feet high, and so it was possible for the dog to pull a mounted horseman off his horse during battle. There are many tales in Irish mythology of their ferocity and bravery in battle.

Apart from their use in battle, these great beasts were also used to guard property and cattle, as well as hunting Irish elk, boar, and wolves. They were a status symbol which, together with the wearing of saffron and having a personal piper, constituted the traditional visible signs of Irish nobility. They were much coveted and were often given as gifts to important personages and foreign nobles. In fact the first written mention of the Irish Wolfhound appears in a Roman manuscript dated 390 A.D. when Quintus Aurelius mentions[4] a gift of seven Irish dogs which "all Rome viewed with wonder".

Other recipients over a thousand years later were the Great Mogul Emperor Jehangier, the Shah of Persia and Cardinal Richelieu. Large numbers were sent to Spain, and King John of Poland is said to have contributed to their near extinction in Ireland by procuring as many as he could lay hands on. Consequently, in 1652, Oliver Cromwell banned the exportation of hounds from Ireland on account of their scarcity.

But the damage was done and the numbers continued markedly to decline through the 18th century. With their natural prey non-existent (the Irish elk and boar had long since been hunted to extinction and the last wolf said[5] to have been killed by a Mr. Watson in County Carlow in 1786), the Irish wolfhound had become an ornamental accessory rather than a hunting dog. Complaints abounded that they were reduced in size, had been made coarse by being crossed with Great Danes, or so crossed that no two dogs seemed alike. By the Irish famine of 1845-6 Irish Wolfhounds were for all practical purpose extinct. There were very few specimens available of the old blood lines.

About this time Capt. George Graham of the British Army, took a keen interest in the wolfhound and decided to revive the almost extinct breed. He was able to obtain descendants of a dog said to be the last 'true' example of the Irish Wolfhound. These he bred with Glengarry Deerhounds, and the resultant hybrids with Borzoi and Great Danes. He eventually achieved a dog that bred true to type and which for all intents and purposes corresponded to Arrian's, 4th Century A.D., description[6] as follows:

> The neck should be long, round, and flexible. Wide chests are better than narrow ones. The legs should be long, straight, and well-knit, the ribs strong, the back wide and firm without being fat, the belly well drawn up, the thighs hollow, the tail narrow, hairy, long and flexible with thicker hairs adorning the tip. The feet should be round and firm. These hounds may be of any colour.

Additionally Graham's breed made excellent companion dogs but sadly their life expectancy of only six to eight years was short. They were shown at the Dublin Dog Shows of the 1870's and an Irish Wolfhound Club was established for the breed in 1885. In 1902 this Club presented the Irish Guards with a prize dog called 'Rajah of Kidnal' as a regimental mascot. Promptly renamed 'Brian Boru' this was the start of a tradition for many Irish regiments.

Early London Irish Regimental Mascots

It has been argued[7] that the London Irish Rifles did not embrace the Irish Wolfhound tradition until 1940 when the 1st. Battalion was presented with a wolfhound. However recently discovered Pathé Newsreel footage[8] shows an unnamed Wolfhound (see page 115) leading the London Irish Rifles during the 1916 St. Patrick's Day Celebrations.

Also a report[9] of the 1931 London Irish summer camp in Ulster mention 'Soldier' a black and white dog as the Regiment's mascot.

Tara the Irish Wolfhound

The wolfhound 'Shaun of Ballykenny' was presented to the L.I.R. in 1940. He was nicknamed 'Tara' and soon became the 1st. Bn.'s mascot and the Band's pet. When the Battalion was posted overseas (August 1942), 'Tara' was transferred to the 70th Bn. L.I.R. (Young Soldiers). He died in 1947.

The Case for a Posthumous Pardon

Justice in an army at war is inevitably quick (some might say rough) and 'Tara' was certainly the recipient (some would say victim) of such rough (in)justice from the Army.

The bald facts of the case as detailed on the charge sheet[10] are that, on 31st May 1941, 'Tara' left his commanding officer to go in search of plunder (to wit one chicken). He was found guilty the same day and sentenced to forfeit one week's biscuits.

However Army justice for dogs appeared to allow no plea in mitigation which would have included the fact that in his early days, 'Tara' had been subject to physical abuse by the regiment's cook sergeant. That this white-overalled soldier had cruelly struck the dog on the nose as he tried to sample the ingredients for a meal. That moment of trauma generated in 'Tara' a deep seated psychological aversion to moving white objects.

If an animal psychologist had been allowed to make a submission at 'Tara'a hearing he (or she) would have advised[11] the C.O. that:

> .... Irish Wolfhounds are sweet-tempered, patient, dignified and willing; they are unconditionally loyal. They tend to greet everyone as a friend, so do not count on them being a guard dog. However they may be a deterrent due to their size. This giant breed can be clumsy. Slow to mature, it takes two years before they are fully grown.

This is an analysis of 'Tara's character that the Band members would have recognised. From the outset they adopted him as their own and they were rewarded with that unconditional loyalty and friendship referred to above. The Band's reciprocation of his loyalty and friendship was tinged with a huge dollop of self interest – when a scapegoat (or rather 'scapedog') was required for the Band's latest 'shenanigans' there was 'Tara' just waiting to be patted by the Band, blamed by the authorities and of course unable to defend himself.

The story is often told[12] of the church parade where the C.O. was about to bring the men to attention. The cautionary part of the command 'London Irish' had been given and every ear was awaiting the word 'Rifles' to spring to attention. Before the C.O. could bark the command, there came a sharp loud yap allegedly from 'Tara'. Eyewitnesses reported that the Band immediately sprang to attention as one. The RSM was not at all pleased and in a voice that all could hear asked "how long had that ****ing dog been the Band's C.O.?" It is not disputed that the bark came from the vicinity of the Band but was it the dog? Could the

Tara the Wolfhound Mascot of the London Irish Rifles, with handler George Jackson and P/M Franklin, 1940.

discriminating auditory sensors of highly trained musicians mistake a dog's yap for a C.O.'s bark?

But to return to 'Tara's' hatred of moving white objects. Apart from literally petrifying the cook sergeant whenever their paths crossed, 'Tara' was soon[13] retrieving female underwear from clothes lines and chasing light coloured doves and pigeons. The Band were 'lateral thinkers' before the term was invented, and soon saw the potential to liberate white chickens from local farms and lay the blame at 'Tara's' paws. In an era of very strict rationing, chicken was a true luxury. Few pipers went on leave without a dressed chicken in their pipe case, first having scattered the plucked feathers around 'Tara's' abode. To assuage their guilt the real culprits invariably made a big fuss of the dog. 'Tara' came to associate white feathers with an extreme display of affection toward him.

So on that fateful day in May 1941, the potent psychological mix of hatred (of moving white objects) and the need for affection (as associated with white chicken feathers) came together. Whilst leading a route march, 'Tara' saw something white moving. Both apprehensive and elated he ran towards a great flock of chickens in a nearby farm. Minutes later he rejoined the march with a chicken in his mouth to seek the Band's now customary affection.

Up until then, the C.O. had resisted calls to discipline 'Tara' for the considerable number of chickens that had disappeared without trace - except for the feathers in the vicinity of the Regimental Mascot. But now there was with a *prima facie* case for 'Tara' to answer. Justice for the dog was instantaneous, without representation, and without regard to anything other than the most basic of facts. In modern parlance this was 'an unsafe conviction'. Clearly a case nowadays for a posthumous pardon.

Dennis Mulqueen – 'Tara's' Handler
Although Dog Major George Jackson led 'Tara' on parade, from the outset Piper Dennis Mulqueen was responsible for the dog's care.

Dennis enrolled[14] as a territorial in the London Irish Rifles in 1932 but did not join the Band as a learner piper until 1937. His civvy street employment was as footman/valet to the German Ambassador and included in his duties was the care of the Ambassador's dogs. Col. Macnamara was aware of this when 'Tara' was offered to the Regiment and ordered Dennis to pick up the young dog from the kennels. From then until the 1st. Battalion was posted overseas Dennis cared for 'Tara'.

After being wounded by mortar fire at Catina, Italy in 1943, Dennis was attached to the Commandant of Military Prisons in Italy until the end of the war. On demobilisation he returned to the London Irish Rifles and after twenty one years continuous service as a territorial he retired in 1953. He then became a very active member of the Regimental Association and when the Association took responsibility for running the Band (see page 67 onwards), Dennis rejoined the Band as a tenor drummer. He was soon appointed the Band's Quarter Master.

Over the years Dennis was a stalwart of the commemorative trips abroad and was a generous sponsor of the cadets' participation in these. His generosity extended to funding the building of Mulqueen's Bar in Connaught House. Band members regard this as his lasting memorial (see page 89).

118

(LEFT)
'Kevin' the Irish Wolfhound
with Dog Major Norman Evans, 1955.

(RIGHT)
Dennis Mulqueen
had a 60 year association with the
Band during which he was a piper,
drummer, dog handler and
quartermaster. He also funded
the building of the bar at
Connaught House.

'Kevin'

After 'Tara', another ten years were to pass before the London Irish Rifles in 1952
once again had a Wolfhound in its ranks. Full name 'Kevin of Ballkelly', his regular
handler was Dog Major Norman Evans.

'Tara II'

In the 1970's, Bugler Dennis Halsey's own wolfhound 'Kipper' served as the Band's
Mascot and was inevitably called 'Tara II'. Such was the impecunious state of the
Band at that time that the dog appeared without the benefit of uniform.

Junior Piper Sean Doyle

The Band's mascots were not always four legged. In 1974 junior piper Sean Doyle
was described[15] as the 'Band's Mascot'. Although only 13 years old he was already
a proven piper and was to become the under 14 Champion of All England. At the
same time, Sean was also the London Amateur Boxing Association's under six
stone boxing champion.

'Tara III'

Although 'Tara III', kennel name 'Solstrand Ross', was owned by Angela Styles, it
was hoped that by classifying the dog as the Mascot of 'D' (London Irish Rifles)

Company The London Regiment, its veterinary and food bill would be funded by the Army. In its infinite wisdom, Whitehall refused to classify the animal as a publicly funded Regimental Mascot and insisted it was a Regimental Pet to be supported by a voluntary fund.

Despite this slight on his status, 'Tara III' was to be a loyal and disciplined Band member from 1998 to 2003. However there were exceptions to his good behaviour! On one parade he took an instantaneous dislike to the cymbal player in the Guards Band and bit him. But his good side far outweighed the bad and he will long be remembered for his seven mile charity walk[16] which raised £200 for The Heart Foundation.

'Tara III' had four handlers whilst he was with the London Irish Rifles. These were Alex Downard and Alan Roberts from 'D' Company and Mark Varga and Les Sheridan from the Band.

Now happily retired, the dog is known as 'Tarka'. This is to avoid any slur on his masculinity by the misinformed thinking he was named after the female lead of 'Gone With the Wind'. In reality all L.I.R. 'Taras' have been named after the Hill of Tara[17] – the political and spiritual capital of Ireland since the late Stone Age and seat of the High Kings until the twelfth century.

(LEFT TO RIGHT)
'Tara II',
with Dennis Halsey, 1973.

Two Legged Mascot,
Piper Sean Doyle, 1974.

'Tara III',
with Les Sheridan, 2000.

References:

1. http://www.armedforces.co.uk/army/listings/l0086.html
2. Hilary Jupp (http://www.irishwolfhounds.org)
3. George Jones (www.barkbytes.com/history/irwolf.htm)
4. op. cit. George Jones.
5. http://www.irishwolfhounds.org/history.htm
6. http://www.irishwolfhoundsociety.co.uk/breedhistory.htm
7. *The Irish Regiments 1683-1999* by R.G.Harris revised H.R.Wilson published Spellmount., 1999. page 256.
8. htttp://www.britishpathe.com
9. *The Northern Whig*, 28th July 1931.
10. www.irishwolfhounds.org/rangers.htm
11. www.doyle.com.au/irish_wolfhound.htm
12 *The Emerald* No.47.
13. *The Emerald* No.47.
14. *The Emerald* No.40.
15. *The Emerald* No.31; page 27.
16. *The Emerald* No.60; page 14.
17. http://encyclopedia.thefreedictionary.com/Tara%20(Ireland)

Band Uniforms

One only has to look at the photographs throughout this book to realise that Band uniforms change over time. Sometimes this has been in a small way; sometimes in an innovative style. Sometimes the aim is to recreate a style from another era and sometimes the revision is in the interest of economy. The following pages review the origins and evolution of the more distinctive items of the Band's uniform. This Chapter is also of use in understanding the Band's Dress Regulations detailed (at page 128) and specific uniforms as depicted in the colour plates at pages 132 and 133.

Pipers' Uniforms

The earliest known photograph of pipers of the London Irish Rifles (see page 9) shows them wearing the Regiment's No.1 Dress Uniform. This was of rifle green with headgear called an Envelope Busby[1] (also known as a Rifle Busby). The busby plume was six inches long and prior to the First World War would have been[2] black and green.

It would appear that the pipers of the London Irish Rifles were not seen in kilts until towards the end of the First World War. It is thought that the idea was copied from the kilted Irish Guardsmen who had come to the L.I.R. in 1916 to learn the pipes (see page 22).

The Pipers' Saffron Kilt

For centuries the common form of dress in Ireland[3] was the 'liene'. This was a loose pleated tunic of linen (the fabric indigenous to Ireland) and made of some 20-25 yards to protect against the cold and cuts and thrusts to the body during battle. The 'liene' could be worn loose down to approximately calf level or, in battle, gathered up at the waist with a belt to increase mobility. The soldiers' 'lienes' were often covered in pitch or with deer skin sewn over it to further the armouring properties of its many pleats.

The 'liene' is recorded[4] in texts by Major in 1521, and Derricke in 1577. Examples of the 'liene' as worn by Irish Warriors can be seen in a 16th century print in the Ashmoleum Museum, Oxford and in similar sketches by Lucas de Heere in 1547 and 1575. The tunic worn by the nobility and very important people was called a 'leine-chroich' or a saffron dyed tunic.

Saffron is a dye/herb obtained from the stigmas of the autumn crocus. It takes nearly 10,000 crocus blossoms to make one ounce of saffron and consequently it has always been very expensive. It is golden coloured and has a strong, exotic aroma and a bitter taste and was in use before the time of Solomon (chapter 4, verse 4) to colour fabric, to perfume people and to flavour food. Later in a 10th Century English Leechbook, (or healing manual) it was ascribed medical properties including protection against vermin.

The Irish nobility (which included the chieftain's piper by virtue of his piping skills) had their garments washed[5] in saffron with a view to repelling lice and imparting a pleasant smell. Repeated washing[6], if you can call four or five times a year 'repeated', increasingly stained/dyed the garment bright yellow rather the dark mustard shade we call saffron today.

(ABOVE)
L.I.R. No.1 Dress Uniform. c1910, as worn by the first pipers of the London Irish Rifles.

(BELOW)
First L.I.R. piper in a kilt? An undated photograph, but a uniform identical to that being worn by the pipers of the Irish Guards in 1916.

The origins of to-day's shade of 'saffron' lies in the 1600's when the colour was 'faked'[7] by soaking garments in a solution of beaten poplar leaves dissolved in urine. Initially the shade was right but darkened with time.

At some stage the 'liene' ceased being a tunic (i.e. pulled over the head) and became a type of wrap around garment (a bit like a Japanese kimono) made of a linen/wool blend. From this evolved the kilt – the lower portion of a wrap over pleated 'liene'. This first appeared in Scotland in the 17th Century and soon crossed over to Ireland. At much the same time linen was becoming very expensive and poorer folk were wearing coarse multi-coloured woollen clothing. The Irish gentry wore saffron for a little longer until they too stopped wearing the kilt and started imitating English dress, although everybody still wore the great cloak.

The Gaelic revival in the 19th Century re-established Irish culture and language but not a national costume. It was not until the Irish regiments had taken up the war-pipes that the question of uniforms (and kilts in particular) emerged. Calling on the experience of the Army's established (i.e. Scottish) kilt makers, and using historic drawings, several versions of an Irish kilt emerged. The kilts of the pipers of the Irish Guards (1916) had an integral apron (like the highland kilt) whilst the original kilt of the Royal Inniskilling Fusiliers (1924) was pleated all the way round. The L.I.R. appear to have adopted the Guards' kilt soon after teaching them the pipes in 1916 (see page 22). Today's kilt is made of eight yards of 19 oz. woollen fabric.

The Pipers' Pouch

When pipers were officially being added to the strength of the Royal Ulster Rifles in 1948, the Full Dress for Pipers included a pocketed day sporran to act as a receptacle for spare reeds, money, wallet etc. The R.U.R. called this item of uniform a 'pouch'.

The pipers of the London Irish who had been assisting the R.U.R. in setting up their Pipe Band, immediately saw the practical value of this pouch and campaigned for its incorporation into their uniform. It was nearly twenty years before these efforts bore fruit and the pouch has been worn by pipers since the mid 1960's.

The L.I.R. piper's pouch is made of patent leather and is suspended on a leather strap. The front is emblazoned with the L.I.R. crowned Tara harp.

The Caubeen & Hackle

The most distinctive sign of an Irish soldier nowadays is probably his head-dress, known as a caubeen from the Gaelic word 'caibin', best translated as 'shapeless old hat'. The caubeen is essentially an oversized beret with a hat band. Whilst there are those who argue that the caubeen is the traditional headgear of the Irish warrior, the only real evidence for this claim is a portrait of Owen Roe O'Neill (c1610), wearing what might be said to be a caubeen.

Khaki caubeens were first worn[8] by the pipers of the Irish Guards in 1916. Originally, in line with all other regiments in the British Army, the badge and hackle were to the left and the caubeen pulled to the right. However for St. Patrick's Day 1921, the Guards C.O. ordered the pipers to turn round their caubeens so that the badge and hackle would be on the right to match the blue plume on the right of the Guardsmen's bearskins.

(ABOVE)
'Irish Distinction',
displayed by a L.I.R. piper wearing a caubeen, saffron kilt and carrying 'Brian Boru' pipes, circa 1923.
Note: Badge yet to be located over the right eye: no brogues or cloak worn.

(BELOW)
The Piper's Plan Pouch
is simply emblazoned with the crowned 'Tara' harp and is in stark contrast to the highly decorative sporrans of the highland regiments.

(ABOVE)
Pipe Major Blackwell, 1932.
Note: The cloak ties cross the chest
before being knotted at the back.

(ABOVE) **The Band's Tunic Buttons**
are silver, embossed with the crowned
heraldic harp of the R.U.R.. Prior to
1969 the Band wore black buttons
with the L.I.R. crest.

(BELOW) **The Cloak's Tara Brooch.**

When the regiments geographically associated with the Irish Free State were disbanded in 1922, the War Office approved[9] uniforms for the remaining Irish regiments which had an 'Irish distinction', including their pipers wearing saffron kilts and green caubeens. Soon, the L.I.R. pipers were wearing caubeens with a blue plume. Initially the badge was over the left eye but the Regiment soon followed the Irish Guards and located the badge over the right eye.

In 1937 the London Irish Rifles extended the wearing of the caubeen to all members of the Regiment but with a green plume – the blue plume being reserved for pipers and officers. The 1930's caubeen was a large symmetrical 'one size fits all' hat. Its girth was reduced by pulling a blue string in the hat band and the L.I.R asymmetrical shape obtained[10] by first soaking the hat in water and then stretching it into the required form over a knee. Plumes were shaped by holding over them over a steaming kettle.

Although the Irish Guards initiated the use of the caubeen, it was the London Irish Rifles who popularised it during the Second World War. During the campaign in Italy (see page 48), where the 2nd. L.I.R. were a battalion of the Irish Brigade, the caubeen's spread to other Irish regiments. Brigadier Pat Scott, who commanded the Irish Brigade, recalled[11] the men:

> began wearing a caubeen type hat but made out of Italian great coats. It was not a very becoming colour, but it was the only material that was available. It was distinctive and it was national.

The Pipers' Cloak

The medieval Irish normally wore a large heavy cloak of woven shaggy wool. This was referred[12] to as the Great Irish Mantle or 'brat' and was often fastened at the neck by a large broach. Unlike its Scottish rectangular equivalent (the 'plaid'), the 'brat' was a tailored semicircle. It was long enough to wrap around the body of the wearer and cover their head if necessary. When not in use the cloak was gathered in and worn over the shoulder, or across the body under the sword arm in battle. In the 16th century, Spencer described[13] the Great Irish Mantle as follows:

> It was their house, their tent, their couch, their target (shield).
> In summer they wear it loose, in winter wrap it close.

When it came to formulating dress uniforms for the Irish regiments in the 1920's, the cloak was the easy part, as it was the only element of Irish dress that had survived the repression of all things Irish over the centuries. However both the London Irish Rifles and the Irish Guards wanted to have St. Patrick blue linings for their cloaks. The competing claims were brought before Field Marshal the Duke of Connaught, previously a Commander- in- Chief of the Irish Regiments. Fortunately for the L.I.R., he had also been their Honorary Colonel since 1871 (see page 28) and it is said[14] that he dismissed the Guards' claim with the statement that "before your regiment was formed, my regiment [i.e. the L.I.R.] had obtained its first battle honour".

The L.I.R. cloak is held in place by ties affixed to it. Originally these ties crossed the chest before being knotted behind the back (see photo of Pipe Major Blackwell above). Nowadays a concealed fixing is achieved by these ties being immediately taken under the armpit after coming over the shoulder. The Tara brooch and chain on the cloak is merely for decoration.

The Drummers' and Buglers' Uniforms

As an operational part of a rifle regiment, the original London Irish buglers of 1860 would have worn the Regiment's 'Sardinian Volunteer Grey' uniform with green facings, dark silver lace and a shako with a green cock's feather plume. After the Cardwell Army Reforms of the 1870's the uniform was of 'Rifle Green' with a spiked cloth helmet of the same colour. Between 1906 and 1914 the Regiment (and hence the buglers) was wearing the 'Rifle Busby' topped with the Regiment's black & green plume.

No record can be found of the Regimental Band's original uniform. But like the bands of other regiments, the L.I.R. Band tended to augment and elaborate the standard uniform. For Queen Victoria's Diamond Jubilee Procession in 1897, this augmentation consisted[15] of green and black piping to the tunic, the drummers had 'wings' of dark and light green with fringing, and black and green drummers cords across the chest.

Around the turn of the century, the Band wore the peakless 'Brodrick' head-dress, but by 1906 this was starting to be replaced with the peaked 'Forage Cap' fashionable with other bands. (Note the mixture of head wear in the photograph on page 13.) This cap was to remain in use by the Regimental Band (including its drummers) until the 1930's.

In 1937 the 'Rifle Busby' (but with an all green plume) was re-introduced to the Regiment as part of the Dress Uniform for buglers and drummers. This uniform remained unaltered until:

- the caubeen replaced the busby (mid 1950's);
- silver drummer's cords replaced black/green cords (mid 1960's);
- drummers' shells to the shoulders ceased to be used (mid 1980's).

The re-establishment of the Bugle Corps in 1992 (see page 97) saw the reintroduction of the rifle busby particularly for military parades. However caubeens are still sometimes worn by buglers and drummers where the public might confuse the L.I.R. Bugle Corps with the Green Jackets. Nowadays the busby's hackle is regimental green except for the Bugle and Drum Majors who wear a St. Patrick's blue hackle.

From the start of the Regimental Band in the 1860's the Bass Drummer wore a leather apron – a tradition that was to be followed until the end of the Second World War (see photograph on page 91). Immediately after the war the Bass Drummer wore a leopard skin trimmed with green edging. During the 1970's and 1980's animal skins tended not to be worn and nowadays the 'leopard skin' used is synthetic and edged with red.

Drummer's/Bugler's No.1 Dress Uniform.
TOP: in 1937
MIDDLE: in 2002

Note: The silver cords, buttons and chin strap in 2002; also the presence of epaulets in place of drummers' shells.

(BELOW)
1932 and the drummers are still wearing peaked caps.

(TOP) **Piper's Caubeen Badge,** is similar to the original (see page 1) but with South Africa in a scroll beneath the harp.

(MIDDLE) **Bugler's Busby Badge,** is a small version of the regimental caubeen badge.

(BELOW) **Bass Drummer's Apron.** In 1946 a leopard skin replaced the leather apron worn for over 80 years by the L.I.R. bass drummer in both the military and pipe bands.

The Band's Badges, Buttons and Belts

The Regiment's original 1860 shako badge (see page 13) was an eight pointed silver star surmounted by a crown; in the centre was a garter inscribed 'Irish Volunteers' enclosing a crowned 'Tara' Harp (as opposed to the Heraldic Harp as featured on the Royal Standard). In 1878, the badge for the newly introduced spiked cloth helmets was a bronze Maltese Cross bearing a crowned Irish harp in the centre and the title 'London Irish Vols' surrounding it (see page 92). In 1902 the Royal crown was replaced by the Imperial crown and the inscription revised to 'London Irish Rifle Volunteers'.

In 1903, the hat badge became a simple crowned harp and silver metal shamrocks were added to the collars of the dress uniforms.

From the start of the Regiment the shoulder-belt plate worn by officers consisted of a crowned 'Tara' harp within a wreath of shamrock. This was designed by Samuel Lover, a founder member of the Regiment who was a great Irish poet and author. It has been reported[16] that despite being 62 years old, he attended all drills with great enthusiasm.

A piper's hat badge was introduced at the same time as the caubeen and this was based on the Samuel Lover 'crowned harp and shamrock design. (see page 1). This piper's badge was to remain in use until the 1960's when the current badge was introduced. This is the same as the original but with the words 'South Africa' (the regiment's first battle honour) included in a scroll below the harp.

When the wearing of the caubeen was extended to the entire regiment (including drummers and buglers for the first time), the regimental cap badge (see page 1) was used. During the Second World War, however, all band members wore the piper's caubeen badge. For a short period after the war, the drummers reverted to the regimental badge but soon the large pipers badge was once again being used by all band members. This remained the case until the 1990's. Since then, when wearing a caubeen, the drummers and buglers have worn the regimental caubeen badge.

The waist belts worn by L.I.R. pipers originally had plain open rectangular buckles, whilst the drummers had the rifleman's 'snake' buckle. By the outbreak of the Second World War the Pipe Major's buckle was a highly decorative solid piece, featuring the crowned 'Tara' harp and a wreath of shamrocks. This remained the *status quo* until the 1970's when all pipers were issued with a solid emblazoned buckle but only featuring the crowned 'Tara' harp. By the early 1980's an emblazoned buckle was worn by all Band members but using the R.U.R. crowned harp and a *'Quis Separabit'* scroll. In the 1990's the decoration on the pipers' belt buckles was changed back to the L.I.R.'s simple crowned 'Tara' harp. Drummers and Buglers still wear the R.U.R. buckle.

When the Band ceased to be the responsibility of the Army in 1969 (see page 67) the traditional rifleman's black buttons ceased to feature on the Band's uniforms. To commemorate the bond that existed with the Pipe Band of the Royal Ulster Rifles, all L.I.R. Band buttons are of a silver finish and are embellished with the crowned heraldic harp of the R.U.R.

Black leather brogues with silver buckles are worn by the pipers. Originally the buckles were plain but since the mid 1970's they have featured a decorative shamrock motif. Drummers and buglers wear regulation black 'George' army boots.

Pipe Banners and Ribbons

For centuries pipers have carried the Arms of their Clan Chief on their drones in the form of a Pipe Banner. When pipers joined the ranks of the British Army, this practice was encouraged, and since the 19th century pipers in Full Dress have carried regimental banners.

The original L.I.R. pipe banners were presented to commemorate the five famous Irish infantry regiments disbanded with the creation of the Irish Free State in 1922. These banners were dark green with black and green fringing. On one side of each banner was embroidered the L.I.R. badge and the then principal battle honours. The five reverse sides displayed a badge of one of the disbanded regiments.

During the Battle of Britain, additional banners were made by Mick Groves, a superb bugler in the 1st. Bn. Band who took[17] his sewing machine to war. He used captured German Parachutes as the bases of these banners and they were decorated with the red cross of St. Patrick. Added to these banners were the various Coats of Arms of the towns in Kent in which the Battalion had served. These Crests were embroidered by the local women's associations.

In 1977 the valuable and potentially fragile pre-war and Second World War banners were effectively laid up and 26 new pipe banners were sponsored[18] by well-wishers of the Regimental Association's efforts to sustain the Band. These banners were made by Mrs A Sainsbury, sister of Dennis Mulqueen (see page 118). On both sides of the new banners is a two inch wide red St. Patrick's Cross on a white background. Around the banner is an edging of entwined dark green and silver strands. On the outside, as carried by the piper, is a silver wire regimental badge mounted on a dark green cloth; this is set above the intersection of the red cross of St. Patrick.

(ABOVE)
An Original Pipe Banner
is on the ground in front of the bass drum. World War Two Banners, made of captured German parachutes, are on the pipes in the back row.

(BELOW)
A Current Pipe Banner
first used in 1977.

(ABOVE) **Pipers' Dirks**
were first issued, at the start of the
Second World War, to the Pipe
Major and the five Company Pipers.
After the War, only the Pipe Major
wore the dirk.

(BELOW) **The Regimental Mace**
replaced the Bugle Major's
Ceremonial Cane from 1975.

Periodically banners are presented to commemorate a person or an event and the Band nowadays has an extensive collection (see back flap of the jacket for examples).

Until the 1960s all pipes were set off with green ribbons. At that time they were changed to the St. Patrick's blue that is used today. During wartime pipe ribbons did not last long and replacements were hard if not impossible to obtain. During the First World War, London Irish Riflemen took small cuttings from pipe ribbons as it was considered[19] good luck to carry a piece of green when going into battle. This sentiment was reflected in Rfn. Frank O'Neill's lyrics for 'A Wee Bit o' Green' which was set to music by Piper Sam Aarons.

St. Patrick's Blue

Over the decades the hue and intensity of the St. Patrick's Blue used by the London Irish has varied. The pipers' hackles were originally a darkish blue, the shade being somewhat similar to the background of the Presidential flag of the Irish Republic. In Irish civic heraldry such a blue is described[20] as St. Patrick's Blue. However in 1939, Col. Macnamara adopted the British Army's version of St. Patrick's Blue, a much lighter shade of blue as used for the plumes of the Irish Guard's bearskins.

In recent times the blue used has been darker, and there are those who remember the lining of the pipers' cloaks being much lighter than today's.

Bugle Major's Cane or Drum Major's Mace

Occasionally after 1970 the traditional Bugle Major's cane was replaced by a mace. In 1980 the Regimental Mace became a permanent feature at the head of the Band. The reason for this has been lost but one of the following is the likeliest explanation.

- After the Association took responsibility for the Band in 1969, it was to an extent funded by undertaking public engagements on a scale it had not seen before. The audiences the Band was now playing to were used to seeing bands being led by a drum major carrying a mace. The idea of a bugle major with a cane was alien to the public at large and it has been argued that the L.I.R. Band gave the public what it expected.

- Alternatively, and equally plausible, is the idea that outside of a parade ground environment it is difficult to see the signals given by a thin, some might say nondescript, bugle major's cane. It has been argued that, particularly on packed carnival parades, a drum major's mace is more visible.

Whatever the reason, the final quarter of the 20th Century saw the Band normally led by a Bugle Major (sometimes called a Drum Major) carrying a Regimental Mace. However, the re-emergence of the L.I.R. Corps of Bugles in the 1990's saw the return[21] of the Bugle Major's cane.

The new Millennium saw both a Bugle Major and a Drum Major on the Band's strength. At present the Band is normally led on parade by a Drum Major carrying the Regimental Ceremonial Mace and wearing the green Regimental Sash which details, in silver thread, the Regimental Battle Honours. The Bugle Major (with cane and sword) normally parades with his buglers. However, in the absence of the Drum Major, the Bugle Major assumes his traditional position in front of the Band.

DRESS REGULATIONS (2004) FOR THE PIPES & DRUMS OF THE REGIMENTAL ASSOCIATION OF THE LONDON IRISH RIFLES

Pipers
(see colour plate no. 2)

Head-dress:	rifle green caubeen; cloth top pulled over left side of head; silver piper's L.I.R. badge over right eye; St Patrick's blue hackle.
Tunic:	rifle green cloth with silver piping and silver facings, fastened by seven equally spaced silver buttons on black facings edged with silver piping; silver piping to epaulets and collar; silver shamrock collar badges; each cuff has three vertical bars of double silver piping, each ending in an emblazoned small silver button; piper's insignia worn on the right arm, midway between the shoulder and elbow; single shamrock worn on left arm, midway between the shoulder and elbow.
Waist Belt:	black leather or patent leather; silver L.I.R. regimental badge centred on solid buckle;
Kilt:	saffron solid colour; resting just above the knees; free side of apron adorned with two green rosettes (the lower one bearing a silver harp, the higher a shamrock).
Pouch:	plain patent leather pocketed day sporran, with silver regimental badge centred on front.
Cloak:	rifle green exterior with St. Patrick's blue silk lining; fixing achieved by ties coming over the shoulder and taken under the arm pit and knotted at the back; decorated with a silver Tara brooch and chain on right shoulder.
Socks:	rifle green ribbed socks with patterned turnover; saffron flashes.
Footwear:	black leather brogues with ornamental (shamrock patterned) silver buckles on black detachable flaps.

Pipe Major
(see colour plate no. 3)

as Piper above but with:

1. silver lace replacing the silver piping on the tunic;
2. additional lace round the top of the cuff;
3. shamrock wreathed pipes above four silver chevrons, the apex of the chevrons to be four inches above the cuff.

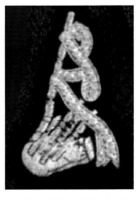

(ABOVE) **The Pipers' Insignia** was originally worn on the right forearm. Nowadays it is worn on the right upper arm.

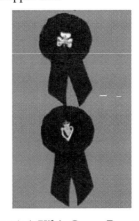

(ABOVE) **A Kilt's Green Rosettes.**

(BELOW) **Pipe Major's Insignia** of shamrock wreathed pipes above four chevrons.

(ABOVE) **The Drummers' Insignia.**

(BELOW) **Waist Belt Buckle**
as worn by the Pipers.
It is emblazoned with the
L.I.R. Regimental badge.

(ABOVE) **Shamrock Collar Badges**
worn by all London Irish Riflemen
since 1903.

(BELOW) **Drum Major's Insignia**
of a shamrock wreathed crowned
drum, above four chevrons.

Drummers

(see colour plate no. 4)

Head-dress: varies as to the nature of the parade. It is either:

a) a rifle green caubeen as per piper but the standard
regimental badge and a green hackle.

or

b) a black rifleman's busby with silver chin strap;
small regimental badge on a circular green background,
with a green plume.

Tunic:	rifle green cloth; fastened by five equally spaced silver buttons; two breast pockets fastened by two small silver buttons; black piping to epaulettes and collar; silver shamrock badges to collar; drummer's insignia worn on the right arm midway between his shoulder and elbow.
Cords:	silver dress cords, worn off the uppermost jacket button (before buttoning the jacket); the leading end passes under the right armpit through the right epaulette and via the second uppermost button, is attached to a cotton loop sewn under the left epaulette near the outside of the shoulder.
Waist Belt:	black leather or patent leather; silver R.U.R. regimental badge centred on a solid buckle.
Drum Sling:	black leather or patent leather, worn under the right shoulder epaulette – the silver buckle and belt end worn either side of the cords.
Trousers:	rifle green.
Footwear:	black leather 'George' army boots.

Drum Major

(see colour plate no. 5)

as Drummer above but with:

1. the Regimental Sash replacing the drummers dress cords.
   The sash is worn under the left epaulette and outside the
   right hand side of the waist belt. The regimental badge and
   battle honours on the green sash are embroidered in silver;
2. a shamrock wreathed drum worn above four silver chevrons,
3. a light infantry sword and sword belt;
4. black leather gloves;
5. St. Patrick's blue hackle or plume.

Bass Drummer
(see colour plate no. 6)
as Drummer but with a full artificial leopard skin edged in red.

Buglers
(see colour plate no. 7)
as Drummer but with:

1. the bugler's insignia replacing the drummer's insignia;
2. green bugle cords slung over the right shoulder under the epaulette; shortened from the regulation issue by plaiting so that the top of the bugle is in line with the bottom of the tunic;
3. a short sword;
4. black non slip gloves.

(ABOVE) **The Buglers' Insignia.**

(BELOW) **Bugle Major's Insignia** of crossed bugles above four chevrons.

Bugle Major
(see colour plate no. 8)
as Bugler but also with:

1. crossed bugles worn above four silver chevrons;
2. a black leather officer's cross belt worn under the left epaulette. The satchel is emblazoned with the Regimental crowned harp and worn centred on the shoulder blades;
3. Light Infantry sword and sword belt;
4. St. Patrick's Blue hackle or plume.

References:

1. *Military Head Dress* by Robert H Rankin, Arms & Armour Press; Hippocrene Books, 1976.
2. *The Emerald* No.15: Recollection by Capt. Pat King.
3. www.royalirishrangers.co.uk/uniform.htm
4. http://home.earthlink.net/~rggsibiba/html/galloglas/gallohist.html
5. *Irish Pipers in the Reign of Henry VIII* by Frank Timoney.
6. www.reconstructinghistory.com/fenians/safron.html
7. *De rebus in Hibernia gestis* by Richard Stanihurst, published 1584.
8. *The Irish Regiments 1683-1999* by R.G.Harris revised H.R.Wilson published Spellmount, 1999; page 97.
9. http://www.reserve-forces-london.org.uk/Units/1107/history.htm
10. *The Emerald* No.53.
11. http://www.reserve-forces-london.org.uk/Units/1107/history.htm
12. www.royalirishrangers.co.uk/uniform.htm
13. www.royalirishrangers.co.uk/uniform.htm
14. *The Regimental Centenary* published by the London Irish Rifles Regimental Association, 1959; page 62.
15. op. cit R.G.Harris, page 251.
16. op. cit R.G.Harris, page 249.
17. *The Emerald* No.42 page 36.
18. *The Emerald* No.34 page 27 and No.35 page 24.
19. *The Emerald* No.18; a recollection by Philip Curran.
20. http://www.ngw.nl/int/ier/b/bantry.htm
21. *The Emerald* No.51; page17.

Plate 1: The Pipes & Drums of the Regimental Association of the London Irish Rifles 1997

Plate 2: Piper Photograph© Sean Dempsey

Plate 3: Pipe Major Photograph© Sean Dempsey

Plate 4: Drummer Photograph© Sean Dempsey

Plate 5: Drum Major

Plate 6: Bass Drummer

Plate 7: Bugler Photograph© Sean Dempsey

Plate 8: Bugle Major

London, 2000.
The Pipes & Drums lead the London Irish Rifles to Connaught House, its new H.Q. in London.

Canada, 1998.
For the first time, the Nova Scotia International Tattoo included an Irish Pipe band when the Pipes & Drums of the Regimental Association of the London Irish Rifles performed in the massed pipe bands of the Tattoo.

France, 2002.
Dedication of the Pipers' Memorial at Longueval which commemorates the Allied Army pipers killed in the First World War.

Regimental Music

The repertoire of the Pipes & Drums of the London Irish Rifles has evolved over the years as the Band's role and purpose has changed. Originally it provided music to march or drill by, to ease boredom or to raise morale. During both World Wars it was common for the Regiment to sing, or shout along with the Band, especially on long marches. Consequently folk songs or music hall ditties were often played. In recent times the Band's catalogue has been augmented with more theatrical music for its auditorium performances.

The Original Music of the London Irish Rifles

In the forty years before the London Irish Rifles took up the pipes, its Military Band (see page 13) was developing the repertoire of Irish standards that remain the musical heart of the Regiment to this day. This included:

'Garryowen'
'Believe me, if all those endearing young charms'
'Oft' in the Stilly Night',
'The Minstrel Boy'
'Brian Boru'

The first L.I.R. pipers were an integral part of the Regimental Military Band and would have been expected to play in unison with the other instruments - hence the need for 'Brian Boru' bagpipes (see page 15). When the 'stand alone' pipe band was established inevitably the tunes it played were straight transfers from the L.I.R. Military Band.

'Garryowen', The Regimental March Past

For centuries 'Garryowen' has been the march that accompanied Irish soldiers going into battle. Eyewitnesses in the early 17th century repeatedly describe[1] how the Irish warriors were led by their pipers to the tune of 'Garryowen'. Many have claimed to be its composer and at various times in its existence[2] 'Garryowen' has been:

- a popular song entitled 'Auld Bessy' (1788).
- an aria in the opera 'Harlequin Amulet' (1800)
- dance music listed in *Campbell's Book of Country Dances* (1800)
- the Regimental marching song of Custer's U.S. Seventh Cavalry (1868-76), when[3] 128 of its 800 or so troopers were Irish.

As is usual with a good pipe tune it was appropriated by the Scots and appeared in Part Two (1802) of Nathaniel Gow's four volume *Complete Repository of Original[4] Scotch [sic] Slow Tunes*.

The London Irish Rifles have never played 'Garryowen' as a slow air. On its formation in 1859, the L.I.R. adopted 'Garryowen' as a march from the 18th Foot (Royal Irish Regiment). A rifle regiment's march past should be played 140 paces a minute and while formally part of the Army, the L.I.R. Band regularly achieved this. Nowadays the Regimental Association's Band plays it at a more leisurely pace, some would say for aesthetic reasons, others so as to accommodate the more elderly members of the Band!

Thomas Moore's 'Irish Melodies'

The existence today of a catalogue of traditional Irish folk music owes much to the work of Thomas Moore (1779-1852). His ten volume opus, *Irish Melodies*, published over a period of 30 years, recorded in print tunes that had been part of the oral tradition for centuries. Although noted for his music, his poetry was equally celebrated and his volumes of Irish Melodies included lyrics he had written for many of the traditional tunes. In due course his *Irish Melodies* was translated into every European language, including Hungarian and Russian.

It is said[5] that at the time his reputation equalled that of Byron and Shelley. In 1817 he was paid £3,000 pounds, then a record, for his poem 'Lalla Rookh'. Despite his vociferous Irish nationalist politics, he had been friends with Robert Emmet whilst at Trinity College, Dublin, Moore was popular at Court and counted the Prince Regent among his patrons. He turned down the post of 'Irish Poet Laureate' because he felt it would require toning down his politics.

Moore's work popularised Irish music throughout the world. Over a million copies of the sheet music for 'The Last Rose of Summer' were sold in the United States alone. His publications were was so popular that he earned £500 annually from them for more than 25 years.

From the start of the London Irish Rifles in 1859, its Band played many of Moore's compositions, most notably 'Believe Me, if all those Endearing Young Charms', 'Oft in the Stilly Night' and 'The Minstrel Boy'.

'Believe me, if all those endearing young charms';
The Regimental Slow March

This slow march is played on 'Retreat' and 'Inspection'. It is usually combined with 'My Home'.

The melody of this slow air was first printed in 1737 to accompany the poem 'My lodging is in the cold ground' but is probably much older. In 1808 Thomas Moore wrote the following lyrics for his beloved wife who had some ghastly skin condition and feared that her husband would no longer love her:

Believe me, if all those endearing young charms,
Which I gaze on so fondly today,
Were to change by tomorrow and fleet in my arms,
Like fairy gifts fading away.
Thou would'st still be adored as this moment thou art,
Let thy loveliness fade as it will,
And around the dear ruin each wish of my heart
Would entwine itself verdantly still.

It is not while beauty and youth are thine own,
And thy cheeks unprofaned by a tear
That the fervor and faith of a soul can be known,
To which time will but make thee more dear;
No, the heart that has truly loved never forgets,
But as truly loves on to the close,
As the sunflower turns to her God when he sets,
The same look which she turned when he rose.

136

Colonel Macnamara is laid to rest, Forli, Italy, 1944.
The piping contingent, to the left, is instantly recognisable by their large caubeen badges and light hackles.

'Oft' in the Stilly Night'; The Regimental Lament.

During the Second World War the lament 'Oft in a Stilly Night' was played at night to signal 'Lights Out' and, the circumstances of war permitting, was used to accompany the burial of a fallen colleague. Nowadays, whenever possible the L.I.R. Regimental Association still provides a piper for the funeral of a former member of the Regiment.

The following emotive lyrics were put to this stirring lament by Thomas Moore; the military variants are in square brackets:

> Oft' in the stilly night,
> Ere slumber's chains have bound me,
> Fond [proud] memory brings the light
> Of other days around me.
> The smiles, the tears of boyhood years
> The words of love then spoken,
> The eyes that shone, now dimmed and gone,
> The cheerful hearts now broken.

Chorus
> *Thus in the stilly night,*
> *Ere slumber's chain has bound me,*
> *Fond [PROUD] memory brings the light*
> *Of other days around me.*

> When I remember all
> The friends [pals] so linked together,
> I've seen around me fall
> Like leaves in wintery weather.
> I feel like one who treads alone
> Some banquet hall deserted,
> Whose lights are fled, whose garlands dead,
> And all but he departed.

Repeat Chorus

137

'The Minstrel Boy'

This traditional air, originally called 'The Moreen', had words[6] put to it by the poet Thomas Moore as a memorial to two friends who died in the 1798 uprising. Nowadays it is normally played as a march in 4/4 time. The poignant words of the first two lines are often used at the funerals of soldiers of Irish regiments. The complete lyrics are:

> The Minstrel Boy to the war is gone
> In the ranks of death you will find him;
> His father's sword he hath girded on,
> And his wild harp slung behind him;
> "Land of Song!" said the warrior bard,
> "Tho' all the world betrays thee,
> One sword, at least, thy rights shall guard,
> One faithful harp shall praise thee!"
>
> The Minstrel fell! But the foeman's chain
> Could not bring that proud soul under;
> The harp he lov'd ne'er spoke again,
> For he tore its chords asunder;
> And said "No chains shall sully thee,
> Thou soul of love and brav'ry!
> Thy songs were made for the pure and free,
> They shall never sound in slavery!"

(ABOVE) **The Minstrel Boys, 1998,** participate in the Annual Parade to Commemorate the Irish Regiments disbanded in 1922.

(BELOW) **Piper Archie McMaster,** missing from the above photograph, has been a Band stalwart for over 30 years. He is also famous for his singing and was once a highland games champion for his voice.

The 'Brian Boru' Yell
was very popular with the 1st.
Battalion L.I.R. during the First
World War as its Pipe Band led
them through France playing
their 'Brian Boru' pipes
(see page 16).

'Brian Boru', The Original 'Connaught Shout'

Originally 'Brian Boru' was a favourite march[7] of the Connaught Rangers during the 19th Century. The tune was played when the Rangers were feeling the strain of a long march and the men's spirits needed reviving, or when the Regiment was marching through a town. On such occasions, during a two second pause in the Band's playing of the tune, the Sergeant-Major led all ranks in a shout[8] of 'Hurroo!' After the shout, the band resumed the tune until the next pause.

At a later date, the march 'Killaloe' (see page 142) replaced 'Brian Boru' as the 'Connaught Shout'.

During the First World War the London Irish Rifles adopted 'Brian Boru' as its 'Regimental Yell' and during the Second World War used it as 'Reveille' to start the day.

Wartime Additions to the Band's Repertoire

Although the poems of such as Rupert Brooke, Wilfred Owen, and Siegfried Sassoon are often presented as 'the literature' of wartime, the lyrics of popular songs were particularly important in keeping up morale. Some songs were overtly nationalistic, such as 'It's a Long Way to Tipperary'. Others were popular because they evoked a sense of nostalgic sadness and loss. Perhaps the most famous such song for the London Irish Rifles was 'The Londonderry Air'. There were also the out and out marching tunes, for which there were as many derogatory lyrics as there were Battalions. For Irish regiments 'Killaloe' was the most notable of these.

'It's a long way to Tipperary'

The song was first heard in a wartime setting by a *Daily Mail* correspondent in Boulogne (18th August, 1914) as a company of the 7th Battalion Connaught Rangers passed singing, " ......with a note of strange pathos in their rich Irish voices, a song that the reporter had never heard before".

The song was 'It's a long way to Tipperary' and it was to become one of the most popular tunes among the British, German and Russian armies during the First World War. It sold a million copies of sheet music in 1914 alone and was later recorded by John McCormack.

Whilst the sheet music of the song shows Jack Judge and Harry Williams as the composers, the circumstances of its composition and who exactly was involved has, over the years, been the subject of much debate.

Recent research[9] reveals that Jack Judge was a music-hall entertainer of Irish stock but he himself had never been to Ireland. On January 30, 1912, Jack was performing at The Grand Theatre, Stalybridge, Cheshire with his younger brother. After the performance, he went to a club near the theatre. It was there that someone challenged him with a bet that he could not write a new song and then perform it on stage during the next performance. The bet was for five shillings, which in those days was the price of a bottle of whiskey and 70 cigarettes.

After leaving the club, Jack heard a fragment of a conversation between two men, one of whom said to the other "It's a long way to........." in the course of giving directions to a location. Jack seized upon that phrase as a song-title, and then added the word "Tipperary". [Some, including L.I.R. Piper Martin Nolan, have suggested it started out as "Connemara" but no decisive corroboration can be found.]

Before going to bed, Jack thought about this idea for a song and then 'slept on it'. In the morning, he quickly wrote the song and got Horace Vernon, the musical director of The Grand, to write down the musical notation as he listened to Jack sing his song.

A long way to Tipperary
for the Pipes & Drums of the
1st. Bn. the London Irish Rifles
in Kirkuk, Iraq, 1943.

140

Jack won the bet when he sang 'It's a Long Way to Tipperary' for the first time, on the stage of The Grand on 31 January 1912, with musical accompaniment led by Horace Vernon. The song quickly became a favourite, and its catchy tune soon caught the public's imagination. But Horace Vernon was not to benefit from the 'collaboration'. The published music lists Jack Judge and Harry Williams as the composers. So who was Harry Williams?

Whilst Jack Judge was an entertainer in the evenings, he tried to make ends meet by running a fish stall during the day in Oldbury. Here the local pub, 'The Malt Shovel', was run by Harry Williams, and he often lent Jack money when trade was poor. In return Jack promised that if he ever wrote a best-selling song, he would put Harry's name on it. Jack kept his promise and both men received a fortune from the song's royalties.

The world famous lyrics are:

> Up to mighty London came an Irishman one day,
> As the streets were paved with gold, sure ev'ry one was gay,
> Singing songs of Piccadilly, Strand and Leicester Square,
> Till Paddy got excited, then he shouted to them there:
>
> *Chorus*
> *It's a long way to Tipperary,*
> *It's a long way to go,*
> *It's a long way to Tipperary,*
> *To the sweetest girl I know!*
> *Goodbye Piccadilly! Farewell Leicester Square!*
> *It's a long, long way to Tipperary,*
> *But my heart's right there!*

> Paddy wrote a letter to his Irish Molly O',
> Saying "Should you not receive it, write and let me know!
> If I make mistakes in spelling, Molly dear", said he,
> "Remember it's the pen that's bad, don't lay the blame on me".
>
> *Repeat Chorus*

> Molly wrote a neat reply to Irish Paddy O',
> Saying "Mike Maloney wants to marry me, and so,
> Leave the Strand and Piccadilly, or you'll be to blame,
> For love has fairly drove me silly – hoping you're the same!"
>
> *Alternative Chorus (often used in wartime):*
> *That's the wrong way to tickle Mary,*
> *That's the wrong way to kiss!*
> *Don't you know that over here, lad,*
> *They like it best like this!*
> *Hooray pour le Francais!*
> *Farewell, Angleterre!*
> *We didn't know the way to tickle Mary,*
> *But we learned how, over there!*

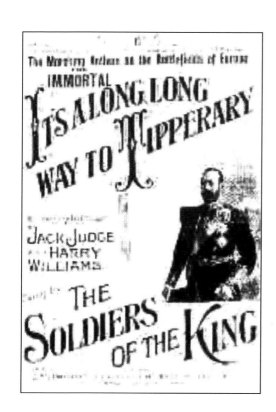

Getting Ready to Shout? (1999).
The L.I.R. Band before the Annual Parade to Commemorate the Irish Regiments disbanded on the formation of Eire.

'Killaloe', another 'Connaught Shout'

This tune was written[10] in 1887 for the musical 'Miss Esmeralda' by an Irish composer named Robert Martin. The melody was made well known in military circles by Lt. Charles Martin, a cousin of the composer, who was serving with the Connaught Rangers at the time. His new set of lyrics celebrated his Regiment's fame and incorporated the 'Connaught Shout', originally used with the tune 'Brian Boru' (see page 139). 'Killaloe' soon replaced 'Brian Boru' in the Connaught Rangers' affection.

Over the next fifty years the march became popular among other Irish Regiments, often with lyrics that were none too complimentary.

The first known recording of 'Killaloe' was made in Northern France by the B.B.C. shortly before the evacuation of Dunkirk. The outside broadcast included, in the words of Richard Dimbleby[11], "a Famous Irish Regiment" playing (and shouting) as they marched past him. The regiment was not named in the interest of national security, but it could not have been the London Irish as they had yet to see action and were still billeted in the UK.

During the approach to Cassino in 1944, the BBC again recorded 'Killaloe'; this time the pipe band was identified as that of the Royal Inniskilling Fusiliers. By then it had been unofficially adopted as the march of the now famous 38th (Irish) Brigade which included the 2nd. Battalion L.I.R.

Sixty years later, 'Killaloe' audiences world wide are still thrilled by this stirring March. All shout at the appropriate point.

'The Caubeen Trimmed with Blue'

The London Irish Rifles gave the world the four part march known as the 'The Caubeen Trimmed with Blue', but as with most pipe tunes it owes more than a little to earlier melodies.

In 1939, when the Second Battalion of the London Irish Rifles was formed, the Regimental Pipes & Drums were split into two so that each Battalion was able to have its own band. The resultant piping strength of the 1st. Battalion Band was very poor and it was decided[12] to advertise for within the Battalion for riflemen willing to learn the pipes. The response was quite good and soon the newcomers were progressing.

To make the lessons stimulating for the learners and their instructors it was decided that everyone should learn a tune from scratch. After searching some books of pipe tunes, a four-part tune called 'Miss Mense's Polka' was found. This, with slight amendments, was easy to learn and enjoyable to play. In another book the same tune was named 'The Liberty Girls' Pipe Band'.

One day, after inspecting the Pipes & Drums, Lt.-Col. Macnamara complimented the Band and expressed his delight with the tune. Piper Mick Nolan told the C.O. that his mother used to sing a song very much like the tune and it was called "I have a bonnet trimmed with blue". The C.O. said: "That's it! We'll name it 'The Caubeen Trimmed with Blue'".

For the 1st. Bn.'s Festival of St. Patrick (1940) words were put to the tune by Cpl. Galway and L/Cpl. Tennyson (a grandson of Alfred Lord Tennyson, the famous Victorian poet laureate). These lyrics were printed on the back of the Festival's programme as follows:

I have a caubeen trimmed with blue
Good St. Patrick's favourite hue.
I have a lass in Dublin town,
Her raven hair comes tumblin' down.
See me march my kilts awhirl
Under my arm the Warpipes skirl.
Cock me eye at a lilywhite hand
Waving to the pipers' band.

Men from Antrim, Derry's men
Men from Naas, and a Connemara glen.
Men from Cork and old Kildare
North and South united here,
First in love but first in war
Sweethearts yo'll see us no more.
Feuds forgotten; factions too,
United by a plume of blue.

Caubeens Trimmed with Blue.
Pipers Alsop and Riley find an amphibious landing in Venice, 1945, quieter than their Anzio landing eighteen months earlier.

".....the pipes, the pipes are calling, from glen to glen and down the mountainside."
(LEFT TO RIGHT)
Chris Burt, Pat O'Brien and Mick O'Malley at Camino, Italy, 1978.

'The Londonderry Air'

This tune is also known as 'Danny Boy' and was very popular during and immediately after the Second World War and is still regarded as a tearjerker.
The melody was collected[13] by George Petrie and published in his *Ancient Music of Ireland* (1855). The untitled melody was supplied by Miss Jane Ross of County Londonderry, who claimed to have taken it down from the playing of a piper in the County. Thus the origin of the name.

'Danny Boy' is one of over 100 lyrics put to the melody. In 1910 Frederic Weatherly, an English lawyer and an enthusiastic composer, wrote an unsuccessful song called 'Danny Boy'. In 1912 his sister-in-law, resident in the U.S.A., sent him the music for 'The Londonderry Air' and he immediately noticed that his original 'Danny Boy' lyrics fitted the melody perfectly. 'Danny Boy' was republished using as its melody 'The Londonderry Air':

> Oh Danny boy, the pipes, the pipes are calling
> From glen to glen, and down the mountain side
> The summer's gone, and all the flowers are dying
> 'Tis you, 'tis you must go and I must bide.
>
> But come you back when summer's in the meadow
> Or when the valley's hushed and white with snow
> 'Tis I'll be there in sunshine or in shadow
> Oh Danny boy, Oh Danny boy, I love you so.
>
> And if you come, when all the flowers are dying
> And I am dead, as dead I well may be
> You'll come and find the place where I am lying
> And kneel and say an 'Ave' there for me.
>
> And I shall hear, tho' soft you tread above me
> And all my dreams will warm and sweeter be
> If you'll not fail to tell me that you love me
> I simply sleep in peace until you come to me.

The Band's Repertoire in the 21st Century

Since the Regimental Association took control of the Band in 1969, it has regularly undertaken interior theatrical performances. Consequently its repertoire is not solely simple melodies to march to or drill to; it also contains complex music that can capture the attention of an audience and generate deep emotions in them. This requires a high degree of technical competency – way beyond the standard of piping demonstrated by Pipe Major Albert Starck's in his early 20th century gramophone recording[14] almost 100 years ago.

Nowadays a performance by the Band is likely to comprise of virtuoso examples of solo piping, intricate drum beating, bugle calls and ensemble playing by the entire Band. These features are comprehensively demonstrated in the Band's performance of 'The Last of the Great Whales'.

'The Last of the Great Whales'

Written by Andy Barnes and subtitled 'The Great Leviathan', at the last count there were over 75 recordings of this modern folk tune including the famous version by the Dubliners. However the composer still regards the original recording of the complete lyrics by Bryony as the definitive version.

The rendition of the tune by the London Irish is based on the original arrangement for the pipes by Captain Chris Attrill (R.I.R. Director of Music) augmented with bugle parts arranged by L.I.R Bugle Major Roy Clarke (see page 97). The intertwined melodies are underpinned with drumming arranged by L/Cpl. Oliver Mason (see page 109).

The lyrics of *The Last of the Great Whales (The Great Leviathan)* are the copyright of Friendly Overtures Ltd.

Bugle Calls

Since the revival of the Bugle Corps in the Band of the London Irish Rifles (see page 97), bugle calls have once again become an integral part of the Band's repertoire.

A bugle call usually comprises of two parts. First the 'regimental' (or 'battalion') call to identify which unit is to obey the command signalled; followed by the 'duty' call which indicates the command to be obeyed. e.g. 'lights out'.

The Regimental call of the London Irish Rifles was based on 'The 'Londonderry Air', whilst that of the current London Regiment is based on 'Oranges and Lemons'. The first official list of British Army 'duty' bugle calls was published in 1798, and many of the most familiar ones, such as 'Reveille' and 'The Last Post', have stayed virtually unchanged since 1815 when they were standardised throughout the realm.

Musical Publications

Further information on the traditional repertoire of the Pipes & Drums of the London Irish Rifles can be obtained from *The Brigade Book of Irish Pipe Music*, first published by the North Irish Brigade in 1949. The lyrics of the Regiment's marching songs are detailed in the 1944 publication *Songs of the Irish Brigade*.

References:

1.   http://home.earthlink.net/~rggsibiba/html/galloglas/gallohist.html
2.   www.emeraldqru.com/seanac501/gaelige.html
3.   *Saga Magazine* September 2003.
4.   the italicised word *Original* are the authors' indication of irony.
5.   http://www.contemplator.com/history/tmoore.html
6.   http://cityofoaks.home.netcom.com/tunes/TheMinstrelBoy.html
7.   http://ezpiper.pwp.blueyonder.co.uk/RIRTunes/ Killaloe/killaloe.htm
8.   'Hurroo' is derived from huzzah which was a sailor's cheer or salute first used in the the 16th Century and was still in use as late as 1839 in Charles Dickens' *Oliver Twist*. By the mid 19th Century the literary form had become *hurrah* whilst in the vernacular it was appearing as *hoorah*, *hooray* and, particularly in Ireland, *hurroo*. This was the form used during both World Wars by the London Irish Rifles as their 'Yell' when the marches 'Brian Boru' and 'Killaloe' were played.
9.   homepage.tinet.ie/~tipperaryfame/longway3.htm
10. www.royalirishrangers.co.uk/music.htm
11. www.iol.ie/~ipba/killaloe.html
12. *The Emerald* No.59; back page.
13. www.theoriginofdannyboy.com
14. www.besmark.com/irish.html

The Regimental Military Band, 1912
with pipers to the rear. Originally they were expected to play in unison with the rest of the Band – hence the use of the keyed 'Brian Boru' pipes.

(Photograph courtesy of Tony Burgess.)

St. Patrick's Day Parade and The Wearing of the Green

St. Patrick's Day 1916.

The symbolic nature of wearing shamrock in the British Army has changed over the centuries and this chapter is devoted to the history, meaning and importance to the London Irish Rifles of its annual St. Patrick's Day Parade and 'The Wearing of the Green'.

St. Patrick's Day Parades

The first recorded[1] St. Patrick's Day Parade was in 1762, when Irish soldiers of the British Army marched through New York to celebrate the Saint's day and their country of origin.

This was to be a short lived tradition in the British Army. The republican uprisings in America and France, which began in 1775 and 1789 respectively, ultimately led to the removal of their Heads of State. This rocked Britain to its foundations and displays of nationalism in the British Army by its Scottish or Irish troops was soon to be unacceptable anywhere in the Empire.

The fear that nationalism was synonymous with revolution was to be justified. In 1791, a political group called the 'United Irishmen' was formed. Inspired by French Revolutionary ideals, they sought an equal representation of all people and a radical reform of the legislature. Their emblem was a green banner with the harp on it.

This movement soon became secret and revolutionary. In 1795 it obtained the promise of French help and a major French expedition sailed from Brest for Ireland in 1796. But, beset by December storms in Bantry Bay, no landing was made. The Government moved against the revolutionaries and after a series of minor battles, the United Irishmen stood their final ground at the battle of Vinegar Hill in County Wexford in 1798. The revolutionaries were greatly outnumbered and thousands died under their green banner. From that time forward 'the green' was a symbol of Irish identity[2] and those wearing it, in any form in Ireland, put themselves at risk. Even so, there was not a law against wearing green or growing shamrock, despite the assertion in Boucicault's world famous lyrics[3] for 'The Wearing of the Green', written to commemorate the 1790's uprising:

Oh Paddy dear, and did you hear the news that is going round,
The shamrock is forbid by law to grow on Irish ground.
No more Saint Patrick's Day we'll keep – his colours can't be seen,
For there's a cruel law against the wearing of the green.

In 1867, however, reality mirrored[4] the fiction of the lyrics. Performance of the tune itself was banned throughout the British Empire by the Lord Chamberlain. This was a consequence of the song being sung in Manchester by an armed crowd as it ambushed a prison van taking men suspected of being members of the Irish Republican Brotherhood to prison. After a police officer was fatally shot, the prisoners escaped, never to be recaptured. However three of the ambushers were captured and subsequently executed for the murder.

"It may be St. Patrick's Day, old man, but I think that's going a bit far."
(a "Two Types" cartoon drawn and presented by JON to the 1st. Bn. L.I.R.)

Piper Peter Hall proudly 'Wearing the Green'.
A master carpenter and cabinetmaker, Peter designed and crafted the Officers' Mess and Mulqueen's Bar at the new London Irish H.Q. at Connaught House. He also resited the War Memorial from the Duke of York's.

The British Army take to the Wearing of the Green

Things were to change during the Boer War in South Africa. After the relief of the town of Ladysmith in February 1900, Queen Victoria ordered[5]:

> all her Irish Regiments to wear the shamrock in their head-dress on the 17th instant [March] .... and in future years on St. Patrick's Day as a mark of her appreciation of the daring display by her loyal Irish soldiers in the recent operations near Ladysmith.

This was a military decree of major significance and another step towards acceptance of all the Irish, their cultures, traditions, and religions. It could be argued that it ranked alongside the Acts of Parliament[6] that allowed all the Irish, irrespective of religion, to own land, to practice their faith without fear of civil penalties, to hold all but a handful of public offices and, as late as 1871, to be given the right of admission to the universities.

Never a Regiment to do things by half, the London Irish Rifles were soon to be seen permanently wearing silver shamrock badges on the collars of the No.1 Dress Uniform, as well as temporarily wearing shamrock in their head-dress on St. Patrick's Day as commanded. To this day all members of the Pipes & Drums wear silver shamrock collar badges (see page 125).

The March 'St. Patrick's Day'

The march entitled 'St. Patrick's Day' first appeared in print in Rutherford's Country Dances (1749). However the tune appears to have been popular as early as 1615 when it was known as 'Barbary Bill' or 'Baco & Green'. It was the regimental quick march of the 4th (Royal Irish) Dragoon Guards (a regimental title dating to 1788), and more recently it has served as the regimental march of the Irish Guard's since they were raised by order of Queen Victoria in 1900.

The Tower of London, 2005.
The Pipes and Drums lead the
London Irish Rifles for their annual
St. Patrick's Day Parade.

St. Patrick's Day Parades by The London Irish Rifles

In accordance with Queen Victoria's command to wear the green, the London Irish Rifles have celebrated every St. Patrick's Day since 1900. In peace or at war, no matter where it has been, the Regiment has paraded to celebrate its roots. From the outset Irish music had an important part to play in the Regiment's St. Patrick's Day celebrations. Since they first paraded in 1909, after two years tuition by Albert Stark (see page 15), the Regimental pipers have added an extra Irish dimension.

London Irish Rifleman George Gadsby's diary entry for 17th to 20th March 1918 recounts:

> ...... and amid glorious sunshine we paraded .... to pay honour to St. Patrick. Our regimental band dressed in knickers [knee length trousers] and green cuffed tunics with their emerald ribboned pipes presented quite a peace time scene and our minds were for a short time taken away from the horrors of war, as the sweet strains of 'Killarney' poured forth in perfect harmony.

Seven days later on 24th March 1918 George was captured at Cambrai. He withstood incarceration as a P.O.W. and lived on to be the Regiment's oldest surviving First World War veteran. In 1999 he was awarded the Legion d'Honneur, one of France's highest awards (see page 78). He died in 2000 aged 102.

The St. Patrick's Day celebrations by the London Irish Rifles normally include the ceremonial distribution of copious portions of shamrock to be worn in the caubeen's badge. Sometimes, particularly during war time, supplies from Ireland could not be guaranteed,

The official papers[7] of Sir Winston Churchill reveal that on 18th February 1941 Lt-Col Macnamara (1st. Bn. L.I.R.) wrote to the Prime Minister asking for shamrock for the Regiment to use in their St. Patrick's Day celebrations. No written record of the reply exists! It is believed that the Prime Minister had other

Shamrock Aplenty!
During the Second World War there was a shortage of shamrock but the London Irish Rifles normally managed to acquire supplies. Here, C.Q.M.S. Wally James presents shamrock to the Mayor of St. Albans, 1940.

things on his mind. The Blitz was still raging around him; his negotiations on 'Lease Lend' were drawing to a successful close; and the Germans were overrunning Greece and Yugoslavia.

In such times of shortage, shamrock has been known to appear from the unlikeliest of sources. In 1940, the 2nd. Bn. celebrated St. Patrick's Day whilst stationed in St. Albans. As C.Q.M.S. Wally James later recalled[8]:

> The Mayor of St. Albans and other guests attended, and a horde of Fleet Street Journalists was present to record the event..... From somewhere they produced a basket of shamrock and cornered the Mayor so that I could pin a sprig on his jacket.

The Band's Latest Recruits.
Pipers William Aspinall and Alexander Wilson experience their first London Irish Rifles St. Patrick's Day.

Potential WWI Recruit:
"I'm a Welsh French polisher, work at Swiss Cottage, drink Scotch whisky, and I want to be a London Irish Rifleman."

(found in a regimental scrapbook)

Irishmen by Adoption

Since 1919 the peacetime St. Patrick's Day Parades by the London Irish Rifles have always included members of its Regimental Association (as the Old Comrades Association has been called since 1955). On the Sunday nearest to the 17th March, past and present London Irish Riflemen congregate to parade behind their Band. Reports[9] of the Day tend to end with the words:

> ...... after the March Past everybody dispersed to the various messes where the Day was celebrated in the usual way for a considerable time.

For some London Irish Riflemen, the Day is a commemoration of their "connection with Ireland by birth, marriage, or property", as the Regiment's founding fathers[10] put it 1859. However, as early as the First World War[11], no more than 2.5% of the L.I.R. were Irish born. Thus for the vast majority St. Patrick's Day is a celebration of the comradeship of the London Irish Rifles. A First World War London Irish Rifleman called 'Pluto' Page summed it up when he said[12]:

> We were proud of being Irishmen, at least by adoption.

He went on to recall the story of a Brigadier enquiring of Col. Concanon, the Commanding Officer of the 2nd. Battalion, as to whether all of his men were Irishmen? "Certainly Sir," replied the C.O. "Sgt. Levi, bring the roll".

References:

1. http://www.erafelegance.com.march.html
2. http://www.rooney.org/green.html
3. http://dunne.yi.org/ireland/A_History_of_Ireland In Song.html
4. http://www.pgil-eirdata.org/html/pgil_datasets/authors/b/Boucicault,D/life.htm
5. *The Irish Regiments 1683-1999* by R.G.Harris revised H.R.Wilson. published Spellmount 1999; page 89.
6. *Encyclopedia Britannica.*
7. *The Churchill Papers*; Char 20/27/54-61.
8. *The Emerald* No.47.
9. *The Emerald* No.30.
10. *The Regimental Centenary* pub. the L.I.R. Regimental Association, 1959; page 27.
11. http://www.irishpost.co.uk/email/printer.asp?j=446
12. *The Emerald* No.15.

The Past, The Present and The Future

A hundred years ago there were some twenty Irish Regiments in the Regular and Volunteer components of the British Army. At some stage in their existence, most had a pipe band in their ranks.

Nowadays the Pipes & Drums of the Regimental Association of the London Irish Rifles is one of only five remaining Irish Pipe Bands formally associated with the British Army. The other four are those of the Irish Guards and the Royal Irish Regiment (both officially established Regimental Bands) and those of the Royal Dragoon Guards and the Queen's Royal Hussars (both part time 'unestablished' bands comprising volunteers from the serving ranks of these regiments).

Clearly, over its one hundred years existence, the London Irish Rifles' Pipe Band has survived and evolved into a unique British Army institution. It is the only Regimental Association Band sustaining the history and traditions of an Irish regiment. It is also unique in that it is the only 'civilian' band empowered to function as a Military Band, supporting the Territorial Army responsibilities of the successor unit, namely 'D' (London Irish Rifles) Company, The London Regiment.

'D' Company's current designation apart, the historic, evocative, regimental title 'The London Irish Rifles' will hopefully live on, for the next hundred years, in the Band that is known, throughout the world, as the Pipes & Drums of the Regimental Association of the London Irish Rifles.

153

Index

Presentation Copies

H.R.H. The Duke of York CVO ADC
General Sir Roger Wheeler KCB CBE ADC Gen
Major General Corran Purdon CBE MC CPM

Library Copies
The British Library
The Bodleian Library, Oxford
The University Library, Cambridge
The National Library of Scotland
The Library of Trinity College, Dublin
The National Library of Wales
The National Army Museum
The Imperial War Museum, London
The Society of Antiquaries, London
The Library of Congress, USA
The Regimental Museum of The London Irish Rifles

Subscription Copies
(in alphabetical order)

James 'Bud'ABBOTT
P. J. ARLOW
Mrs E. Keen (nee BARNARD)
Mrs J. F. BARNARD
J. K. BARNARD
J. R. M. BARNARD
Alfred E. BATES
Robin BRUFORD-DAVIES
Eugene BYRNE
A. L. CAMPBELL
David CAMPBELL
H. A. CAMPBELL
W. CASHMORE
George CLARE
Mrs M. CLARKE
John & Isa CORCORAN
Sean DEMPSEY
Brian DOLAN
G. A. DONNELLY
Jerry DONOVAN

Andrew A. EDEN
Edward 'Ted' George EDEN
The EVANS Family
Doug EVENDEN
B. M. FAHY
John FALLIS
Kathleen & Harry FLAHERTY
Angela FOGARTY
Paddy FOGARTY
Sheila Murphy (nee FOGARTY)
Joy GADSBY
George GIBBINS
John GIBBS
Jim & Olga GRAHAM
Martin GRAHAM
Peter G. HALL
Carl HANDLEY
Donald HENCHY
Faye HOBBS
Ian HOBBS

The 21st Century Crest.

Kathleen & Paul HOBBS
Frances HOWE
Ami IBITSON
Richard IRWIN
Bill JACKSON
Bill JACKSON
G. J. JENKINS
P. P. KELLY
Michael KENNY
Maxine & Barry KENYON
Gerald & Vera KING
Barry Gerald & Karen KING
Maurice LINK
Emma Lucy LOUGH
Paul Anthony LOUGH
Eric & Molly LUCKMAN
John McCARTHY
Kevin McCARTHY
Michael McCARTHY
Timothy McCARTHY
Gerard & Andrea McGUIGAN
Maureen McGUIGAN
A. B. MAHER
Philip C. MASON
D. K. MOGG
Liam NAMMOCK Jnr
Liam NAMMOCK Snr
Ray NEWELL
Martin & Janet NOLAN
Rory & Esther NOLAN
Delcie O'BRIEN
Eileen Anne O'BRIEN
Liam & Fiona O'BRIEN
Niamh O'BRIEN
Mena O'KANE
J. PLUMMER
Stella PLUMPTON
Jim POWELL
Bernadette QUINN
R. E. RANDALL
I. S. M. REA
Brenda RICHARDS
G. W. RILEY & P. Doughty
David & Christine ROGERS

Johanna ROSTANT
Louisa ROSTANT
Maria & Terry SANCHEZ
Patrick SANDS
Harold SAXTON
Charles SELF
S. J. SELLWOOD
Jean SETTLE
Brian SHANAHAN
Mrs H SHANAHAN (nee Nicholson)
M. J. SHANAHAN
Les SHERIDAN
Albert SIMMONS
Tom SMITH
T. STURGEON
Jonathan STRANIX Snr. & Jnr.
Pat SULLIVAN
Fr. Liam TALBOT
E. TAYLOR
Iris S.E. TOMLIN
Arnold TOPLEY
Bill TURVEY
Catherine A. VAUGHAN
Eleanor F. VAUGHAN
J. P. VAUGHAN
Michael I. VAUGHAN
Sinead C. VAUGHAN
Carl J. WATKINS
George WATSON
Daisy WATTS
Denise WATTS
Gary WATTS
Samuel WATTS
Marguerite & Ted WELDIN
Roy & Joyce WELLS
Phil WILLIAMS
Alison WILLIS
Amy WILLIS
Deirdre & George WILLIS
E. D. WILLIS
Rose & George WILLIS
Gordon WILLS
Elizabeth Willis & Ralph YOUPA
Louise YOUPA